ISBN 978-1-333-66482-4
PIBN 10532861

English
Français
Deutsche
Italiano
Español
Português

www.forgottenbooks.com

Mythology Photography **Fiction** Fishing Christianity **Art** Cooking Essays Buddhism Freemasonry Medicine **Biology** Music **Ancient Egypt** Evolution Carpentry Physics Dance Geology **Mathematics** Fitness Shakespeare **Folklore** Yoga Marketing **Confidence** Immortality Biographies Poetry **Psychology** Witchcraft Electronics Chemistry History **Law** Accounting **Philosophy** Anthropology Alchemy Drama Quantum Mechanics Atheism Sexual Health **Ancient History** **Entrepreneurship** Languages Sport Paleontology Needlework Islam **Metaphysics** Investment Archaeology Parenting Statistics Criminology **Motivational**

C. H. McCormick

In Memoriam.

Cyrus Hall McCormick

Born February 15th, 1809.

Died May 13th, 1884.

The Riverside Press, Cambridge:
Printed by H. O. Houghton and Company.

Memoir.

MEMOIR.

CYRUS HALL McCORMICK was born February 15, 1809, at the old homestead, Walnut Grove, midway between Lexington and Staunton, in Rockbridge County, Virginia. His parents, Robert and Mary Ann Hall McCormick, of Scotch-Irish descent, possessed great strength of character and natural ability, and held an influential position among the people in the Valley. Thrift and industry had secured to them ease of circumstances in a devout, intelligent, and happy home, and their seven children shared its responsibilities and pleasures. The children were trained to habits of self-reliance and industry, Cyrus, the eldest, being often aroused by his father's call at five o'clock to go to work in the field. In winter he acquired his education at " the old field-school " in the neighborhood.

His parents were remarkably reverent in their observance of the teachings of divine truth; and Cyrus grew up with an abiding sense of duty and right, and a strong hostility to false pretenses, which he could detect with rare discrimination. An unostentatious bearing was the natural result of such a training in a country home, and it continued to mark his character through life.

On Sunday he entered as earnestly into the singing and preaching in the New Providence Church as he did into the work of the week-day, following the plough or tinkering in his father's workshops. There he sang the music and words of beautiful hymns that remained his chosen songs of praise in all the vicissitudes and changes of his career. This early training in industry, honesty, and religious duty was the strongest influence in moulding his character and life. The bent of his mind was from the first towards practical mechanics, and this was developed and strengthened by the surroundings of his life upon a farm, remote from town or city. During those youthful days he spent much time in the carpenter and blacksmith shops, which his father maintained, as was usual then, for repairing the farm implements and doing the carpenter work needed upon the estate.

In these shops, when only fifteen, he made with his own hands a grain-cradle for his use in the harvest field, and over many a broad acre of grain did he swing this primitive harvester of his boyhood, keeping his place with this light and symmetrical cradle among the full-grown and experienced hands in his father's fields. Thus early in life he had a practical experience of the severe toil from which his invention afterwards released millions of his fellow-men.

The first result of his inventive mind was a hillside plough, patented in 1831, for throwing alternate furrows on the lower side, being thus a right and left hand plough at will. Two years later, he invented a superior horizontal self-sharpening plough, which was pronounced a valuable improvement.

Mr. McCormick inherited from his father genius for invention ; from his mother, genius for practical business affairs. This rare combination enabled him to bring to a successful issue the invention which has given him world-wide fame and honor. His father, Robert McCormick, who possessed much genius in the construction of hydraulic, threshing, and hemp-breaking machines, had devised a reaper in 1816, but, like all previous attempts by others, it was a failure.

Time rolled on, but this old reaper, as it lay abandoned near the workshop, was continually under the eye of the young Cyrus, as a reminder of something attempted but not accomplished. He was convinced that the principles upon which his father had experimented, in using upright revolving cylinders provided at their base with knives like sickles, were radically defective, and he proceeded upon a wholly different plan of construction, by operating upon the grain in a mass, with a horizontal reciprocating blade. The old machine of his father, therefore, furnished him no inductive trains of thought in his work, while it acted as a warning of the errors to avoid, and served as an inspiration to success. The idea that grain could be cut by machinery possessed him fully, and he believed there was a way to do it. He continued to think over and work out his idea in that old homestead. He had never been far from home. He had never heard of any experiments in machinery for harvesting grain except his father's. The pursuit of this idea was opposed by his father, who believed his years would be wasted.

There are turning-points in every life, and usually the point which fixes itself in the memory is some minor incident ; though, in fact, that which is called the turning point is not usually a change of direction, but an awakening of consciousness to the possibilities of the future.

Once, when a young man, he was riding on horseback from his Virginia home to a distant foundry in the mountains, with a pattern of the mould-board of the plough he had invented, and which he wished cast in iron, resting on his horse's neck, and, as usual, was absorbed with his unsolved problem of the reaper. On the way he crossed a considerable stream, and midway in it his horse paused to drink. Just then, as he looked up, his eye fell on a fertile tract of land brightened by the sunshine, and the blended thought of the vast future of the country in agriculture, and the possibilities of his invention for reaping grain, struck him. For a moment there filled his mind a dream of success that seemed like a fable, and which in an instant he brushed aside for the hard realities of the present; but in that instant his resolution took more solid form. Who can tell how much of the inspiration of his work sprang from that moment? The fundamental principles of his invention gradually matured in his mind. Then began the work of transferring these primal ideas into wood and iron. Here his training in the use of tools came into service, and in a few months, after repeated effort in combining the relation of the various parts with unfailing ingenuity and patience, he finally produced a machine, fashioning with his own hands every part of it, both in wood and iron, in his father's workshops. It consisted of, first, a vibrating blade to cut; and, second, a platform to receive the falling grain; and, third, a reel to bring the grain within reach of the blade.

This machine, drawn by horses placed at the stubble side of the swath, was tested during the latter part of harvest in 1831, in a field of six acres of oats, belonging to John Steele, situated within a mile of Walnut Grove. It proved to be a success. Its work astonished all who witnessed it. Neither the young inventor nor any of those present seemed to have even an idea of the true value of the work that day begun, — a work destined to revolutionize the whole method of farming, and to open up a limitless domain in this land for cereal productions; making possible the bountiful harvests that have since that day taxed the powers of transportation, and stimulating the construction of a network of railroads equal to that of all the world beside; as well as wonderfully enlarging the cultivation of wheat elsewhere throughout the world.

A short time after the first trial of the reaper, Mr. McCormick entered into a partnership for the smelting of iron ore. But the panic of 1837, by reducing the price of iron, brought financial ruin to the enterprise. With dauntless courage and unflinching fidelity to creditors, by the united and mutual effort and industry of all his family, they paid all the debts of the firm, though greatly taxing the resources of the family; and he, losing the farm his father gave him, sacrificed everything but integrity.

Disappointed but not discouraged, he turned his thoughts to the reaper, and resolved to devote himself to its improvement and introduction into general use. With very restricted facilities on the farm in Virginia for the manufacture and sale of the reapers, he still worked on there, improving his invention during the brief period of harvest. Soon he realized that the young West was the field on which he might hope for the accomplishment of greater results, and so in 1846 he removed to Cincinnati, Ohio, then a western town, and prepared to build the reapers; for by that time it was well understood that a successful machine had been invented for cutting grain by horse-power. During all these years, while battling with the discouragements always accompanying the efforts to introduce any new machine, Mr. McCormick managed to add improvement to improvement, a work which he kept up during his whole life.

In 1845-47 Mr. McCormick secured additional patents for improvements, which greatly added to the value of the machine, and quickened the demand for it.

The superior advantages of Chicago, as the natural metropolis of an unlimited grain-producing country, soon attracted Mr. McCormick's observation, and thither he removed in 1847. During the following year he there erected substantial reaper works, and built seven hundred machines, increasing the number in 1849 to fifteen hundred. This was an enormous undertaking for those days. In the absence of the improved iron and wood-working machinery of the present day, and with the primitive means of transportation existing throughout the west, where there were scarcely any railroads, more ability was required then to found and foster this industry than now to carry it on in its vastly extended proportions. But Mr. McCormick was a thorough business man, and in addition possessed a spirit of resistless energy and enterprise that faced every obstacle and yielded to no antagonism.

In 1845 Mr. McCormick arranged with a firm in Brockport, N. Y., to build his machine on a royalty, with a view to its introduction into Central New York, then one of the best wheat sections in the country.

After the success of the reaper was assured at home, Mr. McCormick spent some time abroad, bringing his machine to the notice of European agriculturists. In 1851 he attended the World's Fair in London, where his machine was first brought before the British public. During the early weeks of the exhibition, the reaper was the subject of some ridicule on the part of those who knew nothing of its character and capabilities. Even the " London Times " called it " a cross between an Astley chariot, a wheelbarrow, and a flying machine." A few weeks later, however, when the American reaper was practically tested in the English harvest fields, ridicule was turned to admiration, and indifference to widespread enthusiasm.

After prolonged tests, and when the Great Council medal was awarded its inventor on the ground " of the originality and value of the reaper," this same journal made honorable haste to correct its error, and frankly admitted that the McCormick reaper was equal in value to the entire cost of the exhibition. Then, indeed, favors were showered on the inventor. He was prominently recognized, and his acquaintance was sought. From this point his fame grew rapidly, and yet he was as one who knew it not. With his changed status in the world, his heart did not change. His opportunities were enlarged, and he was quick to enlarge his knowledge, and improve by contact with the world of educated men. But his modest, unostentatious nature was not made proud by elevation nor hardened by success.

At the Universal Exposition at Paris of 1855 Mr. McCormick was awarded the Grand Prize for the invention of the reaper, which was " the type and pattern of all other reaping machines of the present day." In 1867 he exhibited his machine at the exposition held at Paris, for which he again received the Grand Prize, and was then decorated by the Emperor with the Cross of the Legion of Honor for his valuable and successful invention.

It is not surprising that a life of such persistent and successful effort as Mr. McCormick's should have been one of continued battle. In this it resembled that of every man who endeavors to supersede the old methods. In establishing his enterprise he found himself surrounded with obstacles well nigh insurmountable, — isolation from centres of communication and trade, insufficient capital, ignorant prejudices of the laboring classes, refusal of Congress to grant him a just and deserved patent protection, and the combined opposition of all other interests similar to his own. Had he not been gifted with indomitable will, invincible courage, and unfaltering confidence in the value of his invention, he must have succumbed to the pressure of adverse circumstances. Instead of this, year by year found him advanced upon the path of progress, and the world bestowed upon him honors and grateful testimonials.

At the same time that this temporal good to humanity was assuming its world-wide proportions, — reaching to the distant peninsula of South America, the shores of New Zealand and Australia, the "pleasant land" of France, the plains of Russia, and the nearer shores of Europe and Great Britain, — a greater but companion work of helping Christ's poor brethren, of the instruction of souls by the proclaiming of Christ's gospel, of shielding and defending the work of Christ's spiritual kingdom on earth, was taken up in the endowment of the Presbyterian Theological Seminary of the Northwest.

It was at the meeting of the General Assembly of the Presbyterian Church, held in the city of Indianapolis in 1859, that Mr. McCormick presented a proposition to endow the professorships, on condition that the seminary be located in Chicago. Its influence in promoting the cause of Christianity throughout the great Northwest is of incalculable value. To this original endowment he has at subsequent times added, as the necessities of the institution demanded. This beneficence has placed the seminary on a sure and permanent basis. Dr. Johnson has impressively said, " How beautiful was the providence that permitted Mr. McCormick, just before the close of his earthly life, to see so rich a fruitage from that sowing. I remember well the evening, only a little while ago, when fifty-nine students of the seminary and a corps of professors, and a circle of friends gathered here where we are gathered to-day, and he sat in the midst of the joyful company, his heart full of intense emotion, and every feature of his face expressive of gratitude to God for the privilege that had been vouchsafed him in sharing so largely in bringing all this to pass."

A religious newspaper, " The Interior," had been started in the city of Chicago to represent the Presbyterian Church. It was struggling in financial difficulty, and its owners applied to him to purchase it. To promote the cause of union between the Old and New schools, to aid in harmonizing the Presbyterian Church in the North and South, to advance the interests of the newly established theological seminary in Chicago, and to promote the welfare of the denomination generally in the great Northwest, were among the objects dear to his heart. So when, in 1872, many friends as well as the owners of " The Interior," urged its purchase upon Mr. McCormick, he willingly assented, and placed it upon such foundation " that it has grown to be a mighty voice, expressing the convictions, the aspirations, and the hopes of a great church."

In 1858 Mr. McCormick married Miss Nettie Fowler, a daughter of Melzar Fowler, Esq., of Jefferson County, N. Y., and niece of Judge E G. Merick, of Detroit. This happy union was blessed with a family of four sons and three daughters, two of whom, a son and a daughter, died in infancy.

Mr. McCormick loved his native State of Virginia with a tenderness that was undiminished with the passage of years. Though he was unable by reason of his important duties in the North and West to be there, except for visits at rare periods, yet he was loyal to her every interest. Her mountains, her valleys, her people, and her institutions of learning were all dear to him.

The Chicago fire of 1871 seriously crippled Mr. McCormick's resources, laying in ashes all his buildings, just as they were beginning to manufacture the supply of machines for the next harvest. But he was almost first to go forward with the work of rebuilding. The reaper works, with every vestige of machinery and patterns, were swept away. He was now advised by many friends to retire from active business, but his reply was indicative of the man, " I know of no better place for a man to die, than in the harness." And so he rebuilt the reaper works on a larger scale than before, and lived to see their capacity increased fivefold.

In 1878 Mr. McCormick was called to Paris for the third time to receive for his reaping and self-binding machine a Grand Prize of the Exposition, and the rank of Officer in the Legion of Honor was then also conferred upon him. He was, at that time, elected a corresponding member of the French Academy of Sciences, " as having done more for the cause of agriculture than any other living man." This recognition of Mr. McCormick's position as a benefactor, through his invention, of the whole race, strikingly corroborates the opinion of two eminent American statesmen, who have left their testimony to the value of the work he accomplished for his native land. In 1859 the late Hon. Reverdy Johnson, in an argument before the commissioner of patents, from testimony taken in the case, said that "the McCormick reaper has already contributed an annual income to the whole country of fifty-five millions of dollars, at least, which must increase through all time." About this time Hon. William H. Seward said, " Owing to Mr. McCormick's invention, the line of civilization moves westward thirty miles each year." For what he accomplished in lessening human toil, as well as for his instrumentality in increasing the means of Christian education, the world recognized his worth, inviting him to high places of honor during his life, and in his death revering and honoring his memory.

In 1878, while at the Paris Exposition, Mr. Mc-Cormick suffered from a dangerous carbuncle on his neck, which necessitated the severest surgical operations, which he bore without the use of anæsthetics. This heroic treatment saved his life, and unusual vigor of constitution and the tenderest care enabled him to rally from this serious illness, after a slow convalescence of five months.

During the next four years, changes of residence in search of climate suited to his condition gave him comparative comfort. While these bodily infirmities were increasing, confining him largely to a rolling chair, so contrary to his former active habits, his mental strength remained unimpaired. Though prevented from moving about in the circles of business, there was no limit to the activity of his mind, and his interest in everything relating to business or social life, domestic or foreign progress, current events of political or national importance, was keen and unabated. While confined largely to the house the last years of his life, his home itself became a business centre. Thither came men from many and varied enterprises and industries, and none left him without having their high impulses and aims strengthened by his counsel and noble example. Here, dictating to his private secretary, following with close and discriminating attention the current events in the world's progress, as the daily journals would be read to him, his mental energies found their congenial occupation. He maintained, to the last, personal knowledge and control of his business, and no important decision, either in the management and extension of this great industry, or in the protection of its legal interests, was made without personal consultation with and direction from him as its head.

On the 22d of April, there were gathered in Mr. McCormick's private room some of the heads of the departments of the McCormick Harvesting Machine Company, and one of his lawyers, Robert H. Parkinson, Esq., to consult upon important questions. The vigor and acumen of Mr. McCormick's intellect in handling these questions deeply impressed them all, and, referring to this occasion, Mr. Parkinson has since written: " I want to tell you what a touching and profound impression I brought away from the interview I had with him not many days before he passed away. Though struggling with the infirmities of age, he took on a kind of majesty which belonged alone to the combination of great mental and great moral strength, and surprised me by the power with which he grappled the matters under discussion, and the strong personality before which obstacles went down as swiftly and inevitably as grain before the knife of his machines. I shall continue to treasure that interview in my memory with grateful appreciation, hallowed by the feeling that his luminous discourse was in some sense a valedictory to business affairs, spoken from the threshold of eternity. I think myself fortunate in having had this glimpse of him, and in being able to remember with so much of personal association a life so complete in its achievements, so far-reaching in its impress, alike upon the material, moral, and religious progress of the country, and so thoroughly successful and beneficial in every department of activity and influence which it entered."

Mr. McCormick's last illness began Wednesday, April 30th, from which he partially rallied Saturday, May 3d, and continued to improve until Wednesday, May 7th, when it became evident that a relapse was imminent, and his nervous strength again began to fail. Not, however, until Sunday morning, the 11th, did the physicians pronounce his case hopeless, nor was it before this apparent to those who watched by his bedside that he would not again rally from this illness, as he had done from other attacks. But the powerful constitution which had carried him through so many critical struggles for life was exhausted, and was at last forced to yield. On the morning of Sunday, the 11th, at six o'clock, the members of the family enjoyed the last moments of his perfectly conscious mental vigor. He seemed to realize that his work on earth was done. Taking the hand of each of his children, he murmured, " Dear one," — then looking at all of them, he said, " My dear children, my sweet children." Finally, taking the hand of his wife, he said, fervently, " Dearest of all — and dearest to all."

One of those near him said, " Do you wish anything?" With great eagerness he replied, " I want nothing now but heaven — heaven before." In answer to other questions, he repeated several times, confidently, and with great firmness, " All right; all right," and again, " All peace." When asked by a friend, who came in, how he was feeling, he answered, " Sweetly." On hearing it said that it was Sunday, and a beautiful day, he answered, " Yes, sweet Sabbath." He knew eternity was just before him, and, knowing this, he was able to be joyful.

He seemed to wish his family close about his bed, and his wife said to him, " My dear husband, we are all here, — shall we have a prayer?" To this he fervently answered, " Oh, yes," and, closing his eyes, while his family knelt at his side, with unfaltering voice he led the last religious service as the head of his family, and made a wonderful prayer, — wonderful, as being the petition of a soul on the verge of eternity, — remarkable for its completeness and strength, and showing the supremacy of his great intellect over nature in dissolution. But its most marked feature was that it was so tender, so submissive. For the last time he lifted up his voice in prayer, and with intellect clear and strong, he commended himself and his dear ones to God. It was like his customary prayers in life, deepened and made thrilling by the time and place, — and ended with "We beseech Thee for the forgiveness of our sins; cause Thy face to shine upon us, lift up Thy countenance upon us, and be gracious unto us, for the Redeemer's sake. Amen;" and then he added, as if in thought, "That name, that name, for *Jesus'* sake. Amen, amen." One of the children then asked him if they should sing his hymn, and he began, with voice clear and strong, to sing the words of his favorite hymn, which during all his life he had loved to sing at family worship : —

> "O Thou, in whose presence my soul takes delight,
>   On whom in affliction I call,
>   My comfort by day, and my song in the night,
>   My hope, my salvation, my all."

In the first verse he sang the air, but in the second he took up a peculiar part, which in his youth he had learned in New Providence Church, Virginia, and which in those days they called "the treble." As the hymn was ended, he repeated, singing over again the last line of the second verse : —

"Or alone in the wilderness rove,"

changing the final word as he sang it for the last time, —

"Or alone in the wilderness *rest.*"

Oh, how sweet that prospect of rest seemed to him !

In the afternoon he had a few lucid moments, though after the early morning hour he was not so fully conscious. During one of these intervals he repeated several times, " Christ, our Spiritual Head."

Sunday night, the attendant physician gave him medicine, and wishing to take this opportunity of giving also some nourishment, then said, " Now you have done your work, you shall have a little food." Quickly he answered, " Yes, work, work," with an emphasis that gave it the importance of a last message.

During Monday he was without pain, and unconscious of the tender care of those around him. The morning of May 13th dawned, gray with misty light, " soft with early showers," and, surrounded by those whom he held in life most dear, he passed from suffering to joy ; from toil to rest ; from death to immortal life.

Funeral Services.

FUNERAL SERVICES.

THE funeral of Cyrus Hall McCormick was held at his residence, 135 Rush Street, Chicago, on Thursday, May 15th, at two o'clock in the afternoon. The day was perfect, and long before the hour appointed a great number of people had gathered at the house.

Just before two o'clock the coffin was placed in the centre of the main hall, followed by the pall-bearers.

Near the head of the coffin the employees of the reaper works had placed a symbol, most expressive of their sense of the loss sustained, — a reaping machine, in white flowers, having the main wheel broken; and the gentlemen employed in the office of the reaper company, in token of their tender regard, placed there a sheaf of ripened wheat, surmounted by a crown of lilies.

The funeral services were conducted by the professors of the Presbyterian Theological Seminary of the Northwest. Addresses were made by

Rev. Dr. Herrick Johnson, Rev. Dr. L. j. Halsey, and Rev. Dr. D. C. Marquis. The opening prayer was offered by Rev. Dr. Thomas H. Skinner, and the closing prayer by Rev. Dr. Willis G. Craig.

The pall-bearers were : —

Charles A. Spring, Jr.	John N. Jewett.
William C. Gray.	William C. Goudy.
Mark Skinner.	Charles S. Carrington.
Henry W. King.	Thomas Drummond.
Horace A. Hurlbut.	Joseph Medill.
Ralph N. Isham.	Murray F. Tuley.

The members of the family present were : —

Mrs. Cyrus H. McCormick, Cyrus H. McCormick, Jr., Miss M. Virginia McCormick, Miss Anita E. McCormick, Master Harold F. McCormick, Master Stanley R. McCormick, Mrs. James Shields, Mrs. Hugh Adams, Hon. E. G. Merick, Eldridge M. Fowler, Mrs. E. j. Carrington, Mr. and Mrs. R. Hall McCormick, Mr. and Mrs. Robert S. McCormick, Mr. and Mrs. William G. McCormick, Mr. and Mrs. Perry H. Smith, Jr., Miss Lucy McCormick, Edward T. Blair, Mr. and Mrs. James H. Shields, Mr. and Mrs. Cyrus H. Adams, Mrs. John E. Chapman, James W. Adams, Mr. and Mrs. H. L. Adams, Miss Ella Adams, Edward S. Adams, Miss Minnie Adams.

THE SERVICES.

HYMN.

My faith looks up to Thee,
Thou Lamb of Calvary,
Saviour divine!
Now hear me while I pray;
Take all my guilt away;
Oh, let me, from this day,
Be wholly thine.

While life's dark maze I tread,
And griefs around me spread,
Be Thou my Guide;
Bid darkness turn to day,
Wipe sorrow's tear away,
Nor let me ever stray
From Thee aside.

When ends life's transient dream,
When death's cold, sullen stream
Shall o'er me roll,
Blest Saviour, then in love
Fear and distress remove;
Oh, bear me safe above, —
A ransomed soul!

The Rev. Dr. Skinner then offered prayer as follows :—

O God, be with us at this hour. May the words of our mouths and the meditations of our hearts be acceptable in Thy sight, O Lord, our strength and our Redeemer. We have gathered here to-day to pay this last sympathetic tribute of regard and honor to Thy departed servant, and then we shall carry him to his own grave, which Thou wilt mark and guard by Thine angels until the trump of the resurrection shall bid us arise in the likeness of the eternal Son of God. Oh be with us by Thy Holy Spirit. May that blessed Spirit hover over our heads as He was over the head of the Lord on the banks of the Jordan, and make this hour a benediction to this afflicted family, and a benediction to all of us who have come to share their grief.

Our Father in heaven, Thou didst give Thy Son to have light in himself, and from all eternity He did live, and then was dead, and then, and now, is alive again. We adore Thee for the gift of Him who is the Light, who is the resurrection and the Life for His disciples. We adore Thee for the gift of Thy Son as our Saviour, by the sacrifice of whose blood Thy justice was satisfied for our sins, and by whose blood our sins are washed away. We desire to give thanks to Thee this day for the hope that we have concerning Thy servant departed, who long years ago stood before Thy people in the world and avowed Thee to be his God and his Redeemer. We adore Thee that he never lost that hope. We adore Thee that in dying that hope cheered him, and heaven opened to his face. Glory to God for a Christian life, and glory to God for a Christian's death! We therefore commit him, his remains and his memory, to Thy keeping, blessed Lord. We shall see him again. We shall meet him by and by. Oh that we might tread the same pilgrimage, and reach at last the bosom of our Lord and Master, there where the wicked cease from troubling, and where the weary are at rest.

And now we desire to commend unto Thee this stricken family. Lord God, thou Incarnate One, who, bending over the grave of Lazarus in death, didst weep, weep with us, O Son of man, for our brother departed, and make this so tender, so precious an hour, that we shall feel that Thou shalt go with us, and dost go with us when we go away from this house of mourning. Bless Thy handmaid, the companion for so many years of Thy departed servant, bound together by the tie which only death can break. Bless her;

give unto her Thy quickening grace, and love blessed Lord. Sustain her in her deep solitude. Guide her in the cares and duties that shall rest upon her when she shall have laid her dead in the grave, and give her grace to the very last to turn to the eternal God, her Saviour in all things. And may these her children be blessed as dwelling with her in this house, and may they give her their support, their sympathy, their obedience, and their love, and may the family be a happy family until death do them all sever. May they be a holy family; may every one of them know Him whom to know is life eternal. Let not one be left out, but all be bound together in the bond of life eternal with the Lord Jesus. And so command thy blessing upon all the kindred, the large circle of natural kinship. God be with them all. May this death be life to every one of them.

O God, what a life it is we live! We come, we stay, we go. Ages have preceded us, ages will follow, and our life is but a hand's breadth in this vast interval. God grant that all of us gathered here to-day may so spend this little span as that when we die we shall be buried with a Christian burial in the hope of a blessed resurrection.

Command Thy benediction upon that portion of the family who have just crossed the great deep, and when they shall know and meditate on this event, quicken their souls by Thy good spirit, and let this death be a benediction to their souls. We commend to Thee all who were associated in industry and work with Thy servant, all that were employed by him in his great earthly mission. God bless them, wherever they may be. Bless those that may be here. Bless all of us without one exception, and grant us Thy presence now, through Jesus Christ. Amen.

SCRIPTURE LESSONS.

God is our refuge and strength, a very present help in time of trouble. Therefore will not we fear, though the earth be removed, and though the mountains be carried into the midst of the sea ; though the waters thereof roar and be troubled, though the mountains shake with the swelling thereof. Selah. For in the time of trouble he shall hide me in his pavilion : in the secret of his tabernacle shall he hide me ; he shall set me upon a rock. Yea, though I walk through the valley of the shadow of death, I will fear no evil: for thou art with me; thy rod and thy staff they comfort me.

For we know that if our earthly house of this tabernacle were dissolved, we have a building of

God, an house not made with hands, eternal in the heavens. O the depth of the riches both of the wisdom and knowledge of God! how un-searchable are his judgments, and his ways past finding out! For of him, and through him, and to him, are all things : to whom be glory forever. Amen.

For a thousand years in thy sight are but as yesterday when it is passed, and as a watch in the night. The days of our years are three score years and ten; and if by reason of strength they be four score years, yet is their strength labor and sorrow; for it is soon cut off, and we fly away. Lord, make me to know mine end, and the measure of my days, what it is; that I may know how frail I am. Behold, thou hast made my days as a hand breadth, and mine age is as nothing before thee; verily every man at his best state is altogether vanity. Selah.

The voice said, Cry. And he said, What shall I cry? All flesh is grass, and all the goodliness thereof is as the flower of the field: they are like grass which groweth up. In the morning it flourisheth, and groweth up; in the evening it is cut down and withereth. The Lord gave, and the Lord hath taken away; blessed be the name of the Lord.

Jesus said unto her, I am the resurrection, and the life : he that believeth in me, though he were dead, yet shall he live : and whosoever liveth and believeth in me shall never die. Believest thou this?

For since by man came death, by man came also the resurrection of the dead. For as in Adam all die, even so in Christ shall all be made alive. But some man will say, How are the dead raised up? and with what body do they come? Thou fool, that which thou sowest is not quickened, except it die: and that which thou sowest, thou sowest not that body that shall be, but bare grain, it may chance of wheat, or of some other grain: but God giveth it a body as it hath pleased him, and to every seed his own body. It is sown in corruption: it is raised in incorruption: it is sown in dishonor: it is raised in glory: it is sown in weakness: it is raised in power. Behold, I show you a mystery: We shall not all sleep, but we shall all be changed, in a moment, in the twinkling of an eye, at the last trump: for the trumpet shall sound, and the dead shall be raised incorruptible, and we shall be changed. For this corruptible must put on incorruption, and this mortal must put on immortality. So when this corruptible shall have put on incorruption, and this mortal shall have put on immortality, then shall be brought to pass the saying that is written, Death is swallowed up in victory. O death, where is thy sting? O grave, where is thy victory? The sting of death is sin: and the strength of sin is the law. But thanks be to God, which giveth us the victory through our Lord Jesus Christ.

But I would not have you to be ignorant, brethren, concerning them which are asleep, that ye sorrow not, even as others which have no hope. For if we believe that Jesus died and rose again, even so them also which sleep in Jesus will God bring with him. For the Lord himself shall descend from heaven with a shout, with the voice of the archangel, and with the trump of God: and the dead in Christ shall rise first; then we which are alive and remain shall be caught up together with them in the clouds, to meet the Lord in the air: and so shall we ever be with the Lord. Wherefore comfort one another with these words.

And I heard a voice from heaven saying unto me, Write, Blessed are the dead which die in the Lord from henceforth. Yea, saith the Spirit, that they may rest from their labors: and their works do follow them. They shall hunger no more, neither thirst any more: neither shall the sun light on them, nor any heat. For the Lamb which is in the midst of the throne shall feed them, and shall lead them unto living fountains of waters: and God shall wipe away all tears from their eyes. And there shall be no more curse: but the throne of God and of the Lamb shall be in it; and his servants shall serve him: and they shall see his face: and his name shall be in their foreheads. And there shall be no night there: and they need no candle, neither light of the sun; for the Lord God giveth them light; and they shall reign forever and ever.

Now the God of peace, that brought again from the dead our Lord Jesus, that great shepherd of the sheep, through the blood of the everlasting covenant, make you perfect in every good work to do his will, working in you that which is well pleasing in his sight, through Jesus Christ; to whom be glory forever and ever. Amen.

HYMN.

How firm a foundation, ye saints of the Lord,
Is laid for your faith in his excellent word ;
What more can He say than to you He hath said, —
To you who for refuge to Jesus have fled ?

" Fear not, I am with thee, oh, be not dismayed,
     For I am thy God, I will still give thee aid :
     I 'll strengthen thee, help thee, and cause thee to stand,
     Upheld by my righteous, omnipotent hand.

" When through the deep waters I cause thee to go,
     The rivers of sorrow shall not overflow ;
     For I will be with thee thy trials to bless,
     And sanctify to thee thy deepest distress.

" Ev'n down to old age my people shall prove
     My sovereign, eternal, unchangeable love ;
     And then, when gray hairs shall their temples adorn,
     Like lambs they shall still in my bosom be borne.

" The soul that on Jesus hath leaned for repose,
     I will not — I will not desert to his foes ;
     That soul — though all hell should endeavor to shake,
     I 'll never — no never — no never forsake ! "

The Rev. Dr. L. J. Halsey then made the following address : —

" Blessed are the dead who die in the Lord, from henceforth, yea, saith the Spirit, that they may rest from their labors, and their works do follow them." How blessed are the Scriptures of God to us all to-day, as a comfort in distress, as a consolation in sorrow, as a welcome voice from heaven, as a message of peace to our stricken hearts from our ascended glorified Redeemer.

And how is this Scripture of the blessed dead who die in the Lord, and rest from their labors, exemplified and fulfilled in the remarkable career, the successful work, the peaceful end, the rounded and finished life of this servant of God, our friend and brother, who is now called from earth to that higher and better world! He is indeed gone from us, but his memorial lives, his record is on high. His life here is ended, but his influence abides, and his works do follow him. In view of such a life, so full of useful work, such a character, so rounded and complete, and such a peaceful, happy death in Christ, we may well feel the nearness of heaven, and with it the divinity of that holy religion and the preciousness of that Gospel, which this servant of God professed. From his early youth, and through his long and active career, he has been a consistent, faithful member of the Church of Christ, and in the strength of those convictions of truth and duty which were inspired by the Word of God, he was enabled to go forward to the end — even until he fully finished the great life-work God had given him to do. Truly may we say, God gave him length of days and he filled them up with works of usefulness.

Whilst, therefore, we are all deeply sensible of

the heavy bereavement and sorrow which such a
death has brought upon this Christian household
— taking from them the beloved husband and
father and friend, who had been their head and
stay so long — whilst our warmest sympathies
are awakened for them, and our tears of sadness
flow mingling with theirs in this great loss, we
must, nevertheless, feel that God has ordered all
things in wisdom and love.   The prominent feeling in our hearts to-day is, that this was a well-
directed and finished service — that this was a life
spent in God's fear, and a character moulded on the
principles of God's Word ; that our loss here is
his eternal gain, and that this friend and brother,
whom we have known as a faithful servant of the
Church of God, a most prominent member of this
whole community, has now but completed his
course, kept the faith, and ascended to his reward.
It is not often that God gives to his children here
the opportunity and the honor of doing so large
a service for the church and for the public good,
and of doing it so well.   Having served his generation by the will of God, he at last rests from
his labors.   But his works and his influence do
follow him.

In many respects Mr. McCormick may be
called a representative man.   Among the busi-

ness men of this growing city, where he so long lived, he was a representative man, identified fully with its business life, its industrial activities, its great manufacturing interests. In these relations, probably no one of our citizens was more widely known and honored abroad. He was a representative man of the Presbyterian Church, of which he was through life a member, and whose welfare he labored so fervently to promote; and not only of his own particular church, but of the whole Presbyterian and Evangelical family of churches throughout the land, in all of which he felt a Christian and patriotic interest. A representative man, too, we may truly say he was, of this whole generation in which he has lived and toiled. Scarcely any man in our day has perhaps done more to increase its wealth and its agricultural resources, and thus to stamp his memory on the living of his own time and on the works of those who shall come after him.

It would not be appropriate now to point out all the aspects of his remarkable career as a man, a citizen, a public benefactor, a world-renowned inventor, and to tell of the influence for good which has gone forth from his life-work in these different channels. I may but barely allude to these wider and more general characteristics and public ser-

vices. Let me come to a nearer view of his
work for the church, and restrict my remarks to-
day especially to that one important work of his
life with which in the good providence of God it
has been my privilege to stand somewhat inti-
mately associated with him for the last twenty-
five years. I refer to the work he inaugurated
in this city a quarter of a century ago, in laying
the permanent foundation of the Theological
Seminary of the Northwest for the training of
young men for the Gospel ministry. With that
remarkable sagacity which ever distinguished all
his business transactions, he had perceived, several decades earlier, that this young and growing
city, of what was then the Northwest, was of all
places in the country the best suited to his purpose for the permanent establishment of the great
reaper works. And what sagacity did it augur
in the man, that at a time comparatively early in
the history of the city, and early, too, in the history of his own individual fortune, he foresaw
with equal clearness, that of all localities this rising metropolis of the Lakes was precisely the
point where the Presbyterian Church most needed
a permanent and fully endowed school of sacred
learning for the education of her ministry, and
the evangelizing of our great northwestern terri-

tory. It was about the middle of this month of May, just twenty-five years ago, at the meeting of the General Assembly in the city of Indianapolis, that he made that great proposition which struck the country with surprise and satisfaction, to donate one hundred thousand dollars for the permanent establishment of a Theological Seminary in Chicago. Other places had eagerly sought the honor, but this liberal offer decided the question. The Assembly accepted the proposal, elected the professors; the institution was opened for students in September, 1859, and was thenceforward identified with the interests of this great city, with the interests of the whole Northwest, and with the interests of this vast interior region of which it is the commercial, educational, and religious centre.

Who can estimate the wide extent and the far-reaching influence of a work like this? I have reason to know that he brought the institution to this place not for the sake of the Presbyterian Church alone, though he was ever a staunch advocate and defender of the church, and sought to promote all the highest interests. But he had wider views and sympathies. He sought to found this institution of sacred learning, not only for the benefit of the church, which he loved so well, but

in the interests of that wider Christianity of which
the Presbyterian Church is but a part, and in the
interests of our common country, North, South,
East, and West. He felt from the first that both
the church and the nation required an institution
of this character just at this point. Nor did he
ever lose faith in the undertaking. Through all
the trials and discouragements of its early history, in the face of apparent indifference and want
of coöperation on the part of the church, and a
degree of odium and misrepresentation on the
part of the public outside, from which many a
man would have shrunk, he went steadily forward
in his purpose ; he " bated not a jot of heart or
hope," and with that firmness and tenacity of will
which characterized his whole life, he resolved
that this Seminary by God's blessing should be a
success. And God spared him long enough to
see these efforts crowned with the most gratifying
success. In the midst of increasing bodily infirmities during the last few years, he seemed to
feel an increasing interest in the welfare of the
Seminary. He was permitted, in the good providence of God, to see the return of this month of
May, — the anniversary of his first gift. During
the intervening years, since 1859, he had added
at different times donations to the Seminary,

amounting to a sum three-fold his original gift, some for buildings, some to increase the endowment fund, and some for other purposes. It seems a remarkable and most fitting close to the great work of benefaction towards this institution, that during these last few years of his mortal life, he added yet another and third munificent gift of a hundred thousand dollars for the erection of professors' houses and a new and more extended dormitory building, — thus covering the Seminary campus with spacious and elegant edifices, lifting the institution out of all its embarrassments, and placing it on a solid basis of assured success and of enduring usefulness. And thus he crowned this last quarter of a century of his active life with a wise and liberal beneficence similar to that with which he had begun it, and similar to that with which he had filled up the intermediate years.

Such is the record of what he had done for this institution, and through it for the whole Presbyterian Church, and for our common country. Surely no institution in our land has ever had a stauncher friend and a more liberal benefactor. It may devolve on others to tell what he has done for our broad land, and for other civilized lands in all parts of the world, as the inventor of one of the most important and useful implements of agriculture known to mankind. While his name will live through coming ages in all the world of fruitful industry, by reason of this labor-saving and almost wonder-working machine; and while his monument will stand here on the other side of the city in that vast manufacturing establishment built up by his business energy and foresight, which is now sending its reapers over the world at the rate of fifty thousand annually, this other monument of his wisdom and benevolence will also stand for all coming time, by which he has associated his name indissolubly with all the best interests of the Presbyterian Church and the Christian ministry.

Certainly his was a privileged and useful life, a successful and wondrously completed work. Certainly it is no small honor which God has conferred upon him and upon those who bear his name, who have shared with him his pilgrimage of active toil, and who, now that his day of life is ended, live to resume the task and carry forward his work. It is a distinction of sacred and blessed influences to have been associated with such a benefactor of the public, such an inventor of useful art, such a friend of institutions of education, such a founder and supporter of the schools of sacred learning.   Not alone has this city of Chicago been the witness and recipient of his benefaction.   In all parts of the country, North and South, East and West, there are those who could rise up and tell of his large and timely gifts to our struggling academies and colleges and schools of the prophets, and to many local churches that he has helped to sustain, and whose financial difficulties he has removed by generous donations.

Blessed then are the dead who die in the Lord when they can rest from their labors after works like these, when they can leave their kindred, their fellow-citizens, and their fellow-Christians, with memorials of good example, of faithful service, of consistent character, and of generous benevolence, such as have marked the history of our departed brother.   It was the grace of God that enabled him to do so well his appointed life-work.   It was God who inspired him with the purpose to do such a work, gave him the means and filled his heart with that tenacity which enabled him at last to make his work an accomplished fact.   Whilst then there is much in the history of this life and in its peaceful, happy end to cheer the heart of the bereaved ones, and to encourage the living to imitate his example, we still feel the sadness of the hour, and deeply sympathize with the stricken family in the blow which has deprived both them and us of such a friend and helper, such a brother and co-worker in Christ Jesus our Lord.

The Rev. Dr. D. C. Marquis then delivered the following address : —

> "There is a reaper whose name is Death,
>   And with his sickle keen
> He reaps the bearded grain at a breath,
>   And the flowers that grow between."

Perhaps only yesterday we gathered the tiny flower that grew between the stalks of ripened grain, and with tearful eyes we buried its withered beauty out of our sight. To-day it is the stalk of bearded and ripened grain, cut down in the fullness of its days; the gathered sheaf, the shock of corn full ready for the garnering. There is something deeply and powerfully impressive in the sight of the strong oak that has towered among its fellows of the forest, lying prone upon the earth, its place vacant, its strength vanished, its life gone, though its usefulness is not ended. We think of the years that giant tree has flourished, of the life it has lived, of the storms it has weathered, of the deep-rooted stability that inspired and commanded confidence, of the strength that has so long afforded shelter and repose ; and when we contrast all this with the prostrate form so still and helpless, the lesson it teaches is the story so often repeated, old as the history of man, and yet ever new and ever needing to be taught again, that the strongest earthly life must reach its close, the most far-reaching and enduring of earthly ties must be severed, the longest and most conspicuous path of earthly activity and influence must have its end.

A scene like this is before us to-day. The life that has gone from among us was no common life. It was the life of one who rose conspicuous among his fellow-men. The name engraved upon this casket is celebrated throughout the civilized world ; the man who dwelt in this clay tabernacle was eminent in his generation. A life of eminence, of influence, of usefulness, of strength, has passed away, and we who were his neighbors and friends are here to pay our tribute of respect to his character, and to give expression to our sympathy with those bereaved, by testifying our sense of the loss which his departure has caused to his family, to the community, and to the wide circle of interests so greatly benefited by his life.

There is always much to be learned from the

record of an earnest, laborious, honorable life. It is profitable to dwell upon the history of one who has achieved eminence and an honorable fame by the force of native qualities of mind, directed by unswerving purpose, indomitable perseverance, and untiring labor. But still more profitable is it when these native qualities, thus trained and thus directed, have achieved their grandest results in closest harmony and truest consistency with those eternal principles of truth and right, which reach beyond time and lay hold upon eternity.

My brethren here have already spoken of the more public life and services of Mr. McCormick. Let it be mine rather to speak of those more personal characteristics, which were the controlling principles of his life; the things which gave to the man his marked individuality and force; and the impressions to which I shall try to give expression are those gathered from the intimacies of personal friendship, from the experiences of that closer companionship which is born of sympathetic association.

There are certain traits of character which Mr. McCormick possessed in an eminent degree, upon which I need not enlarge, for they are known and read of all men. It needs not that I should tell any with whom he came in contact of his un-swerving integrity, of his unfailing tenacity of purpose, of his strength of will, and of his untir-ing perseverance in the pursuit of an object. And yet these are qualities that are liable to be misapprehended, and the man who possesses them is liable to be misjudged. The unthinking world, which knows only what it sees, and which judges a man's life by what appears upon the surface, might attribute these traits of character to pride of will, or obstinacy of disposition. And in some men it may be so. But having been associated with Mr. McCormick in times of trial, I can speak from personal knowledge ; and justice to him de-mands that I should speak it here ; — that the substratum of his character was formed by an underlying principle, deeper, broader, grander, sublimer far than any of those which I have enumerated. That which gave intensity to his purpose, strength to his will, and nerved him for perseverance that never failed, was his supreme regard for justice, his worshipful reverence for the true and the right. The thoroughness of his conviction that justice must be done, that right must be maintained, made him insensible to reproach and impatient of delay. I do not wonder that his character was strong, or that his purpose was invincible, nor that his plans were crowned with an ultimate and signal success; for where conviction of right is the motive power, and the attainment of justice the end in view, with faith in God there is no such word as fail. I do not affirm that he was always accurate in discerning with minutest correctness just where the justice lay, for no man is infallible. But I do affirm that he was firmly convinced that right and truth and justice lay at the goal for which he strove, and with that conviction he was not to be turned aside. And as an evidence that this testimony is true, and that no mere personal gratification was his motive, it is enough to say that, much as we have talked together and planned together about the things wherein he differed from his fellow-men, I never heard him utter one word in harshness toward the absent, nor speak of them in other terms than those which the truest charity would prompt. Speaking directly to an antagonist, his words were sometimes sharp and strong; but speaking of him none could be more gentle, none more charitable than he. And this is a test of Christian principle that cannot easily be gainsaid.

2. Another characteristic of Mr. McCormick was his unquestioning faith. He believed with-

out hesitation whatever was said in the Bible. He had a settled confidence that the whole Bible was the Word of God, and that whatever it said must be true. He also had implicit faith in the sovereignty of God, and the purpose of God, and an abiding confidence in the superintending providence of God. And that is the kind of faith that makes men strong. The spirit born of such faith expects great things and attempts great things. It stops not for fear of failure, but goes on, sure of success. It gives a man decision when he has to choose, and firmness when he proceeds to act. Only let him see that there is a word of the Lord applicable to the case in hand, and there is an end of doubt.

3. Still another distinguishing characteristic of our friend was his love for and his devotion to the distinctive doctrines of the Gospel. He had none of that kind of charity which confounds light and darkness, and truth and error, and imagines that all who profess Christianity mean the same thing, no matter what they say. His charity was of the genuine apostolic kind which rejoices only in the truth. We all know it to be true, and it is with a feeling of utmost thankfulness that I here proclaim it, that no religious teacher, however vast his learning, however bril-

liant in intellect, however attractive in eloquence, or however celebrated in reputation, could ever win this man's confidence unless he taught the great leading doctrines of Christ's gospel with no uncertain sound. Justification by faith, regeneration by the spirit, the propitiatory sacrifice of Jesus Christ, the God-man, the only way of salvation. These and kindred truths were the things he loved to hear clearly stated, and if there was a deficiency here, whatever others might think, he was not satisfied. And, my friends, whatever other things he may have repented, I venture to say he never repented of that, and he does not regret it now.

Take then these three things: his supreme regard for the principles of justice, truth, and right; his implicit faith in the Bible as the Word of God; and his love for, and devotion to, the fundamental and essential truths of Christianity. These principles working upon a resolute will and a sound judgment and a determined purpose, is it any wonder that his character was strong, or that his life was a power, or his measures a success? And yet it was not the cold, stern nature that might be supposed to accompany conscious strength, nor was it the unsympathetic nature that might be moulded by success. The faith he cherished was a faith that inculcates charity, and right nobly has he exemplified it. His gifts have been dispensed with a princely munificence to every cause that in his judgment would promote the temporal, or moral, or religious welfare of his fellow-men. Chastened by suffering, his last days were occupied in strengthening enterprises of Christian beneficence, which he had long felt it a privilege to aid. And when the last hours came, and the earthly interests and duties must be laid aside, it did not meet him as a surprise. He knew in whom he had believed. His last conscious act on earth was to lead his household to the throne of grace, and in prayer commit them to the care of a covenant-keeping God. His last conscious words, as though all backward thoughts were vanished, and only the forward remained, were, " It is ended here ; it is heaven now." And so he fell asleep.

> " Soldier of Christ, well done,
> Praise be thy new employ,
> And while eternal ages run,
> Rest in thy Saviour's joy."

The Rev. Dr. Johnson then delivered the following address : —

If I were broadly to characterize the brother and father whose decease we here recognize, it would be by saying that he was one who put his thought into things, rather than words. He could speak, if there were occasion, with decision and emphasis. Forceful and effective public utterance was possible to him, but he did not lean that way. He was not, by eminence or preference, in oratory the impassioned or the syllogistic reasoner. He rarely took the platform to carry men's hearts by power of pathetic appeal, or to carry their reasons by weight of argument, though he had both imagination and logic ; but commonly his imagination and his logic found other expression than that which is connected with public speech. He directed his effort towards putting his thought into things, rather than into words ; and the things to which he chiefly gave his thought represented three great departments of human interest, — industry, education, and journalism. Born and reared on a farm, it was natural that his thought should first be given to industry ; and the thinking he did there while at the plough and harrow, and while swinging the scythe and cradle, was that kind of thinking which has given to man's hand the capacity of a loom, which has given to his arm the mighty beat of our trip-hammers, which has given to his feet, through the steam-engine, the power of annihilating distance, and to his eye, through the telescope, the sweep of all the stars. Other boys have been born and reared on farms, and have kept on swinging their scythes until themselves mowed down at last by the Great Reaper. Not so with this lad of Virginia. His active imagination early saw possibilities of power in muscles of iron and steel that did not lie in the flexible sinews of his right arm. He married brain to muscle, and, lo! the reaper, which has been steadily, through his oversight and inventive genius, perfecting itself, until now it does for three continents what the cotton-gin does for the South. For a full quarter century it has been attending the world's great gatherings of peaceful industry, where the nations have come together to celebrate the brain's independence, and there it has won trophy after trophy in the battles of peaceful industry, until the medals and prizes and testimonials fairly cluster thick about the man who stood as its animating genius and fruitful inventor. In the providence of God, it seems to me that he was made the hand that reached over and dropped the largest blessing on toil that has ever fallen as a benediction out of heaven. And it is a beautiful and appropriate thing that the workmen of this great business should come to-day and lay their tribute of affection and reverence upon this casket; for the music of the reaper is the sweetest music that is now heard by the ear of industry. This continent is peopled, and railroads are enabled to push their enterprises into its vast inland spaces, because the *reaper* is there to give them the harvest whose gathering would otherwise have been impossible.

But this man of inventive genius, whose bent it was to put his thought into things, did not confine himself to material interests. The value of the reaper may possibly be represented by dollars and cents. Mr. McCormick went higher and deeper, he thought of souls as well as machines. And the thing into which he put this thought as representative of another department of human interests is that Theological Institution of whose founding and career we have already heard, showing that the beloved and honored man was moved by higher considerations than those which simply appeal to selfish interests and to the accumulation of wealth; that into his soul came ideals he would seek to realize by an outward and public expres-

sion. When the Seminary of the Northwest was
a child with few friends, without any foundation,
and with no assured future, he proposed, even in
the pressure of his absorbing business, and while
that business was yet in the comparative dawn of
its great development, to bring the seminary to
Chicago, and give it stability and financial an-
chorage where, in the midst of this great metropolis, and in the midst of this vast inter-continen-
tal region, it might do a great work for God, in
rearing a living ministry.

You have heard the story of his persistent,
faithful, generous, and large-hearted connection
with the institution, without whose agency it
never would have had the wide and conspicuous
and grandly prophetic place it holds to-day in the
heart of the church. How beautiful was the
providence that permitted him, just before the
close of his earthly life, to see so rich a fruitage
from that sowing. I remember well the evening,
only a little while ago, when fifty-nine students of
the seminary and a corps of professors and a circle
of friends gathered here where we are gathered
to-day, and he sat in the midst of the joyful company, his heart full of intense emotion, and every
feature of his face expressive of gratitude to God
for the privilege that had been vouchsafed him in
sharing so largely in bringing all this to pass.

Later on, he discovered another need that came to his eye and heart, in the field of journalism. A religious newspaper, " The Interior," had been started in this city, representative of the Presbyterian church. It was struggling in early darkness and difficulty, when he was led to shoulder the responsibility of its management, and to place it upon such foundation and secure for it such competent editorship that it has grown to be now not an organ but a mighty voice, expressing the convictions, the aspirations, and the hopes of a great church, and destined beyond all question to perpetuate itself through years and ages, into the far distant future.

Now what was behind all this, — what the make-up of such a man doing such a work? I would say that he was characterized, first of all, by great energy, that was capable of marshaling immense resources, and of commanding every possible facility for the furtherance of a great interest, and of pressing them with tremendous force to the accomplishment of any given object. But men sometimes move with great energy for a while, and then lose hope and heart. Not so he. For along with great energy he had great tenacity of purpose, into which he seemed to put the very soul of unalterableness. When he once decided a thing ought to be done, that thing went down, so far as human will could place it there, into the catalogue of things irreversible. If it lay in the realm of possibility, it was done. Then along with this, he had a deathless and dauntless courage, so that he was never appalled by obstacles, never abashed in the face of opposition, and never troubled about difficulties, though environing and threatening him on every side. He was like that Swiss chieftain, to whom one of his followers said, as he was about to step into a boat to cross the lake in a storm, " It is impossible to cross this lake to-night," and to which the chief replied: " I know not whether it be impossible, I know it must be attempted." When Mr. McCormick became convinced a thing ought to be attempted, he was fearless in the face of opposition, no matter what its might or multitude.

But these qualities I have named show simply the man of power. When these are alone they give us the despot, the man of iron heel, the man who can win victories, but win them ruthlessly. Accompanying and regulating these qualities in Mr. McCormick's nature, keeping them mainly to just procedure, was a regnant conscience. And back of all, beneath all, round about all, softening and mellowing the man, was the affectionateness

of a great tender heart. I do not suppose that
the mass of people knew that he had this royal
possession, for he did not " tie his heart upon his
sleeve for daws to peck at." It might have been
better if he had shown a little more of this emo-
tional nature. But as his pastor, and in the intimacies of personal friendship, often and often I
have seen his heart lifted to his eyes until those
determined eyes melted into tenderness and tears.
Often and often I have seen the lighter and mag-
netic side of his nature get such supremacy that at
last, all over the fixed features of his face, it broke
out in ripples of laughter. He carried a great joy
and a great tenderness beneath what, to some,
may have seemed a rough exterior. He was
moved with emotion until tears rolled down his
cheeks, again and again, at some tender exhibition of the truth of God in the sanctuary. He
believed God, and it was accounted to him for
righteousness; and at last, through much suffering, he entered into the kingdom.

> " ' I know ' is all the sufferer saith,
> ' Knowledge, by suffering, entereth,
> And life is perfected in death.' "

Last Sabbath morning, in the early dawn, the
whole family gathered about his bedside, and his

oldest son said to him, " Father, shall we have our morning prayer, as usual ? " " Oh, yes," said the father ; and, with the entire household kneeling around his bed, he led them in prayer, saying his " Amen " with firmness and trust. Then he broke out in a beautiful hymn, in which the family joined : —

" Oh ! Thou in whose presence my soul takes delight."

Then, bidding, one by one, his household goodby, he wrapped the spotless robe of Christ's righteousness about him, and " fell on sleep." Blessed indeed are the dead that die in the Lord. Yea, saith the Spirit, that they may rest from their labors, and their works do follow them.

At the conclusion of these addresses about four hundred employees of the Reaper Works, many of whom have been there for twenty years, and felt a sincere attachment to him, walked in a double line past the coffin to bid a long and sad farewell to their departed leader. The remains were interred in Graceland Cemetery.

Resolutions.

RESOLUTIONS.

——◆——

SARATOGA, *May* 16, 1884.

THE General Assembly of the Presbyterian Church being in session at Saratoga, Elder Thomas Kane, of Chicago, announced the death of Cyrus H. McCormick as having occurred at 7 A. M., Tuesday, May 13, with appropriate remarks upon his work for the church, and offered the following Resolution, which was adopted by the Assembly rising to their feet : —

Resolved, That this Assembly has learned with sorrow of the death of Hon. Cyrus H. McCormick, and recognizes the loss which the church has sustained in the departure hence of so devoted and munificent a friend of Christian and theological education, and of every good work.

GENERAL ASSEMBLY OF THE PRESBYTERIAN
CHURCH IN THE UNITED STATES.

VICKSBURG, MISS., *May* 21, 1884.

The General Assembly of the Presbyterian
Church in the United States, in session in this
city, this day unanimously adopted the following
minute, and ordered the undersigned to forward
the same to you : —

" The General Assembly having information of
the death of the Hon. Cyrus H. McCormick, of
Chicago, Ill., deems it eminently suitable to make
a record of an event which marks the departure
to his everlasting rest of a Christian man, who,
throughout a long life, has consecrated so much
of his ample wealth to the welfare of his fellow-
men. In all these benefactions the people and
institutions of his native south were largely and
most kindly remembered."

JOSEPH R. WILSON,
Stated Clerk.

PRESBYTERIAN THEOLOGICAL SEMINARY OF THE
NORTHWEST.

MINUTE OF THE FACULTY ON THE DEATH OF HON. CYRUS H.
McCORMICK, ADOPTED MAY 24, 1884.

The Faculty of the Presbyterian Theological
Seminary of the Northwest here record upon
their minutes their views and feelings in connection with the decease of the lamented Hon. Cyrus
H. McCormick.

I. The sagacious foresight and wisdom of Mr.
McCormick in selecting, twenty-five years since,
the commanding location of this city as the appropriate and permanent seat of this Institution, and
in making it secure through the action of the
General Assembly of the Presbyterian Church,
by a donation of one hundred thousand dollars.

II. His steadfast conviction of the importance
of maintaining the Seminary in the spirit and
purpose of the action of the General Assembly,
and this when, instead of admiration and gratitude for his sagacity and beneficence, he was con-
fronted with no little opposition and opprobrium.

III. His readiness to come to the aid of the institution amid its difficulties, not only by many

needful gifts at different times, but also by the contribution of another hundred thousand dollars towards its endowment.

IV. Four of the members of the Faculty have special occasion to record their gratitude to Mr. McCormick for his gift of most commodious and beautifully located residences, by which not only their personal comfort is secured, but the Institution itself is benefited by the opportunity thus given for constant oversight and influence in connection with the students.

V. The Faculty hereby express their own and the church's very great indebtedness to Mr. McCormick for his prompt and noble munificence in the erection of the new and spacious dormitory on the grounds of the institution, for the increasing number of students.

VI. We also take this occasion to record our sense of gratitude to Mr. McCormick for the wide door he has opened to each and all of us for usefulness to the church of his and our warmest affections.

VII. And finally we thank God that before his departure from the scene of his large Christian benefactions, he was permitted the gratification of witnessing the most encouraging tokens of prosperity and success in the Institution to which he had given so much thought and labor and bounty.

Resolved, that a copy of this m nute be transmitted to his family, with the expression of our tenderest sympathy in their bereavement and grief, and our prayer is that the God of Consolation may sustain and comfort them as the Husband of the widow and the Father of the fatherless.

WILLIS G. CRAIG, Chairman.

EDWARD L. CURTIS, *Secretary.*

MEMORIAL RESOLUTIONS BY THE EXECUTIVE COMMITTEE OF THE BOARD OF DIRECTORS OF THE PRESBYTERIAN THEOLOGICAL SEMINARY OF THE NORTHWEST

The Executive Committee, on behalf of the Board of Directors, desire to record an expression of their profound sorrow at the great loss sustained by the Seminary and the church at large, in the death of the Hon. Cyrus H. McCormick.

The warm and unfaltering friendship of Mr. McCormick for the cause of education, especially in training young men for the ministry, was shown not only by his words but by his deeds of munificence, which constitute an enduring monument to his memory, and will cause him to be remembered as one of the benefactors of mankind. The Seminary of the Northwest, the good influence of which will be felt through all time in Christian education, will remain as an example of his wisely directed benevolence to be emulated by others.

The timely beneficence of Mr. McCormick to this institution was but an expression of his strong faith in God, and of his love for the highest interests of mankind.

We desire to extend to the family of the deceased our deepest sympathy in their great bereavement.

In the life of such a man, the world can learn lessons from the fidelity with which he improved the opportunities both of youth and manhood, and found time, amidst the cares of the immense industry over which he presided, to ascend to higher levels of thought, and engage in works of philanthropy which will endear his name to coming generations. Through his good works " he being dead, yet speaketh."

SAMUEL M. MOORE, *Chairman.*

DANIEL S. GREGORY, *Secretary.*

PRESBYTERIAN THEOLOGICAL SEMINARY OF THE NORTHWEST.

RESOLUTIONS PASSED BY THE ALUMNI OF THE THEOLOGICAL SEMINARY OF THE NORTHWEST IN SPECIAL MEETING AT THE GENERAL ASSEMBLY AT SARATOGA, N. Y., MAY 18, 1884.

Whereas, in the all-wise providence of God, the Hon. Cyrus H. McCormick has been called from his labors in this life to his reward, be it

Resolved, That we, the Alumni of the Theological Seminary of the Northwest, in special meeting at the General Assembly of the Presbyterian Church, express our gratitude to God for a life so largely useful to the cause of theological learning.

That while humbly submitting to this dispensation of Providence, we mourn the loss of one who has been to the Northwest, and the whole church, a most munificent friend of theological training and Christian education.

That we extend our sympathy to the bereaved family in their affliction and prayerfully commend them to the consolation of the Divine Comforter.

Resolved, That a copy of this action be sent to the sorrowing family, and that it be published in the " Interior " and other church papers.

Rev. W. F. RINGLAND, *President pro tem.*
Rev. JOHN MCALLISTER, *Secretary pro tem.*

WOMAN'S PRESBYTERIAN BOARD OF MISSIONS OF THE NORTHWEST.

Room 48, McCormick Block, Chicago.

At a Memorial Meeting of the Board at its rooms, May 16th, the following resolutions were passed by a unanimous rising vote : —

In the death of Mr. Cyrus H. McCormick the world has lost a helper, and this organization a warm friend and sympathizer, who has been identified with it almost from its commencement. Through his benefaction, " Room 48 " has become a great Mission Centre of America, — therefore,

Resolved, That while we sincerely mourn his loss, we thank our Heavenly Father for his long life of usefulness and generosity, esteeming it a privilege that we were permitted to share his fellowship.

Resolved, That we strive to emulate his noble life of service, so that through us he may continue to raise up many who remain in the dark shadows of ignorance, sin, and death.

Resolved, That we offer to the bereaved family our tender sympathy, rejoicing, in our sorrow, that the husband and father has left them a rich legacy of prayer, which will insure to them the blessing of God, while they entrust all their sorrows and cares to his keeping.

Resolved, That a copy of these resolutions be sent to the family, and published in the " Interior," and entered upon the records of this Board.

Mrs. GEORGE H. LAFLIN, *Secretary.*

WASHINGTON AND LEE UNIVERSITY.

EXTRACT FROM THE MINUTES OF A MEETING OF THE BOARD
OF TRUSTEES, JUNE 24, 1884.

The following paper, presented by Benjamin M. Smith as a tribute to Cyrus H. McCormick, deceased, was adopted, and the Secretary directed to furnish a copy thereof to President Lee, with a request that he communicate the same to Mr. McCormick's family : —

The trustees of Washington and Lee University place on record this

MEMORIAL OF HON. CYRUS HALL McCORMICK.

This eminent Christian philanthropist was born of a pious Scotch-Irish ancestry in Rockbridge County, Va., near the village of Midway, February 15, 1809. He became a communicant in New Providence Church in 1834, and ever continued a consistent professor of the Christian Faith. Having served his generation by a life abounding in good works, he closed his career, full of years and of honors, and fell asleep in Jesus May 13, 1884.

He grew up to adult age on a farm, and notwithstanding the limited advantages generally incident to such a position, by the vigor of a natural intellect of extraordinary endowment, he obtained in a good school a sound and thorough education. He also learned the lessons of a high moral culture and of industrious habits, constituting the basis of integrity and fidelity to duty, which marked his memorable career. His great invention, the Reaper which bears his name, was the result of successful study and careful experiments, and was put on the market in 1839. During forty-five years since, by his eminently judicious management, this invention has spread incalculable blessings over the civilized world.

In Mr. McCormick's character, as developed in his various relations, there have ever been presented true modesty, unflinching moral courage, persistent prosecution of purpose, unwearied industry, indomitable energy, and unblemished integrity. He furnishes a brilliant example for the imitation of young men in every walk of life.

Mr. McCormick's success in life was accompanied by a generous course in behalf of the interests of collegiate and theological education. In the dark and distressing period of the history of this Institution, immediately after the war, he came to its aid with a generous donation of

$10,000, afterwards increased to $20,000. He also
endowed a Professorship in the Union Theological Seminary, by a donation in 1866 of $30,000.
Having by his great invention contributed so
fully to the material prosperity of the Northwestern States, with a wise discrimination and
enlarged pious purposes he determined to increase the ability of a Theological Seminary
theretofore situated in South Hanover, Indiana,
by effecting its removal to Chicago, and greatly
adding to its endowments.

Having succeeded in this plan, he continued his
contributions till they reached nearly $400,000.
He lived to see the number of students reach fifty-
nine, treble the former attendance. By these efforts he conferred on that region of the country
the highest and most durable benefits. " He now
rests from his labors, and his works follow him."

Thankful to the kind Providence for rearing
up such a man, this Board humbly bows to the
orderings of the same wise and holy Providence,
which has removed him from the number of its
members, as well as from that of the valued friends
of the University.

And it was ordered, That a copy of this Memorial be published in the " Lexington Gazette,"

and that the " Christian Observer," the " Interior," and the " Central Presbyterian " be respectfully requested to copy it.

And on the motion of Bolivar Christian,

Resolved, That the President of the University be requested to express to Mrs. C. H. McCormick and her family, the desire of the Board of Trustees to possess a portrait of Hon. Cyrus H. McCormick, to place with the collection of the portraits of patrons of the University now within its walls.

JACOB FULLER, *Secretary.*

LEXINGTON, VA., *June* 26, 1884.

MINUTE OF THE FACULTY OF WASHINGTON AND LEE UNIVERSITY RESPECTING CYRUS HALL McCORMICK.

LEXINGTON, VA., *May* 26, 1884.

The Faculty have received with profound regret and sorrow the intelligence of the death of this distinguished friend of this University and member of its Board of Trustees, and feel it to be their privilege to place on record some tribute to his memory.

Mr. McCormick was one of the justly notable men of his generation. His name is known, not only in every part of our own country, but throughout the civilized world, and wherever known, is mentioned with honor and gratitude, as associated with most beneficent services to the human family. The benefits he conferred on his race are not to be estimated by the value of the great invention that bears his name, merely, but also by the impulse which his eminent success has given to others possessing genius and energy akin to his, in seeking to make improvements in other departments in agricultural machinery. It is not too much to say that no man in all history has achieved so much for the progress of that branch of industry which is universally recognized as the basis of individual comfort and national prosperity.

He was conspicuously a Christian philanthropist. His pecuniary benefactions to the institutions of religion were frequent and liberal, in some instances munificently large. Although for many years of his life residing in a distant State, he did not lose his interest in the land of his birth, or those who were the friends and neighbors of his youth. Union Theological Seminary in Prince Edward County has a professorship named for him in commemoration of his gift of the funds for its endowment.

Our own University, Washington and Lee, being situated in his native county, was not over-looked by him whilst inquiring for objects on which he might bestow his favors. An endowed chair of instruction bearing his name is the appropriate response of the University to his generous contribution to its funds.

To his widow and children we tender our deepest sympathies in their sad bereavement, and our prayers that the Father of all Mercies by his Almighty Grace may be their stay and solace.

A copy.

JOHN L. CAMPBELL, JR.,

Clerk of the Faculty.

PRINCETON THEOLOGICAL SEMINARY.

MINUTE ADOPTED AT THE ANNUAL MEETING OF THE ALUMNI ASSOCIATION

At the Annual Meeting of the Alumni Association of the Princeton Theological Seminary, held in the Chapel of the Seminary at Princeton, May 14, 1884, the following minute was unanimously adopted by the Association : —

News of the death of Mr. Cyrus H. McCormick of Chicago arrests the attention of this Association, which has a mournful interest in putting on record the following testimonial.

Resolved, 1st, That we express our deep sense of the loss the Church has incurred in an event which has removed so wise a counselor and so generous a promoter of Theological Education in the Northwest.

Resolved, 2d, That we thank God for the service and liberality of our departed brother and for his steady attachment and devotion to the church of his father; that we offer our sympathy to those in the South and West most closely associated with him in the advancement of theological education, and especially to the immediate family of the deceased, to whom we respectfully transmit a copy of these resolutions.

WILLIAM E. SCHENCK,
Secretary of the Alumni Association.

LAKE FOREST UNIVERSITY.

RESOLUTIONS ADOPTED AT A MEETING OF THE BOARD OF
TRUSTEES

At a meeting of the Board of Trustees of Lake
Forest University, the following resolutions were
unanimously adopted : —

Resolved, That in the death of the Hon. Cyrus
H. McCormick we recognize the loss to the business world of one whose career has been almost
unexampled in the history of this country, and
which has had few parallels in the history of the
world.

By his death the cause of education also has
lost a friend whose marked liberality in this direction has made his name conspicuous, and who has
left for himself an enduring monument in the Presbyterian Theological Seminary of the Northwest.

His energy in business and his liberality to education were accompanied by trust in God, and
an unwavering faith in the great fundamental
truths and doctrines of the Christian Scriptures
as held by the Presbyterian Church, of which he
was a communicant for half a century.

We deem his life in those respects worthy of emulation, and we place on record our expression of heartfelt sympathy with the bereaved household in this providence.

By order of the Board,

SAMUEL D. WARD, *Secretary.*

CHICAGO, *May* 14, 1884.

CHICAGO HISTORICAL SOCIETY.

Mr. W. H. Ackerman, for the Committee appointed to prepare a memorial notice of the late Cyrus H. McCormick, an annual member of this Society, presented the following, which was unanimously adopted : —

The Chicago Historical Society places upon its records, in loving memory, this brief record of the life of its late member, Mr. Cyrus H. McCormick, who became a resident of this city in the year 1847, and who departed this life on the 13th of May, 1884.

Life to him was a victory in a double sense. Possessed of a wonderful physical constitution, he fought its battles manfully, and overcame every obstacle in working out its great problem ; and not even in later years, when bowed down by the infirmities of the flesh, did he neglect the claims of the higher life. From him the commands of his Master always received a loving recognition, as evidenced by his many liberal contributions to the cause of religion.

He was never unmindful of the duty he owed

to his God, nor was he ever ashamed to acknowledge Him openly before men. He was given to hospitality, as many a poor servant of Christ can testify.

He was a man of superior business capacity, of great determination, remarkable executive ability, and indomitable courage in acting upon his own convictions, and he could not be swerved from a conscientious discharge of what he believed to be duty, when measured by the standard of strict integrity.

He was just and considerate in his relations with all who were dependent upon him for their daily bread, and these gave grateful acknowledgment of the obligation under which they rested in the genuine expression of sorrow on the day of his burial.

He was in every sense a public benefactor — his generous gifts to the church, to the Theological Seminary, and to various benevolent objects will cause many to " rise up and call him blessed."

His inventive genius has given to mankind that which has practically revolutionized farming operations, and established for him a reputation over the entire civilized world.

With him the harvest of life has ended — " the silver cord is loosed, the golden bowl is broken."

He has gone to meet the reward of that Saviour whose cause he so devotedly served while here on earth.

The " dust has returned to the earth as it was," and the spirit has returned unto the God who gave it."

The foregoing is a true copy of the record.

ALBERT D. HAGER, *Secretary.*

INTERNATIONAL COMMITTEE OF YOUNG MEN'S CHRISTIAN ASSOCIATIONS.

Cor. 23d Street and 4th Avenue, New York.

At a meeting of the Committee, held at the office, May 13, 1884, the following minute was adopted : —

It is with profound regret that we, members of the International Committee, learn of the death of Hon. Cyrus H. McCormick, the father of one of our associates and an honored and generous friend of our work. And we desire to express to our friend and brother, and to the members of his bereaved family, our sincere sympathy with them in their irreparable loss, assuring them also of our heartfelt appreciation of the Christian character and preëminent usefulness of him whose loss we mourn, and who is lamented by the great multitude, in this and other lands, who appreciate what he accomplished for the comfort and well-being of his own and every succeeding generation of mankind.

12

RICHFIELD SPRINGS PRESBYTERIAN CHURCH.

RICHFIELD SPRINGS, N. Y., *May* 18, 1884.

The Session of the Presbyterian Church of Richfield Springs passed the following preamble and resolutions : —

Whereas, Our Heavenly Father in his providence has been pleased to remove from the toils and conflicts of the church militant to the fellowship and rewards of the church triumphant, Hon. Cyrus H. McCormick, for many years a resident of this village during the summer, and a constant worshiper with us when able to be present, thus evincing, as well as by his gifts, his interest in the cause of Christ ; therefore

Resolved, That in the death of Brother McCormick this church has lost a true friend and a generous patron, and the church at large one who was deeply interested in the advancement of the Redeemer's kingdom as shown by his large gifts to collegiate and theological institutions.

Resolved, That we commend the family of our deceased brother to the tender sympathies of our common Lord, praying that his grace may sustain them, and his presence comfort them in this time of sorrow.

Resolved, That these resolutions be entered on the pages of our sessional records, published in " The Interior," " New York Evangelist," " Richfield Springs Mercury," and that a copy be transmitted to the family of the deceased.

D. M. RANKIN, *Moderator*.

P. K. HOPKINS, *Clerk*.

HASTINGS COLLEGE.

At the annual meeting of the Board of Trustees of Hastings College, Hastings, Nebraska, the following resolution was unanimously adopted, June 18, 1884: —

Resolved, That we, the Board of Trustees of Hastings College, this day assembled in annual meeting, record our gratitude to God for the munificent life of the lamented Hon. Cyrus H. McCormick, and that we record our gratitude that McCormick Hall, the first building of Hastings College, has been erected as a beneficent monument to his memory.

THORNWELL ORPHANAGE.

At a meeting of the Board of Visitors of the Thornwell Orphanage, Clinton, South Carolina, the following preamble and resolutions were adopted : —

Whereas, On May 13th, Hon. Cyrus H. Mc-Cormick, after leaving an admonition to " Work " to the Church of God, "fell on sleep : "

Resolved, That his life was a benefaction to mankind. By his inventive talent he revolutionized grain-culture, causing millions of heads of wheat to stand where one stood before, thus feeding the nations. His youth was an example of purity, industry, and noble worth, to the youth of all time. His old age was a typical old age, — for his heart was the heart of a child, his head the head of a sage, and his hand was a blessing to his church and his nation.

M Cormick

In Memoriam.

IN MEMORIAM.

More appropriate than this black line, this symbol of mourning, would be a pencil of the setting sun, if it could be transferred to this page in its roseate radiance. The shock of bereavement and grief falls heavily upon the heart. That strong hand lies lifeless. That heart which knew no fear, but was full of all generous emotions, is still. Those keen perceptions, that force and grasp of intellect, that indomitable will, have left the now dark and silent tenement, and have become active and imperishable forces in higher and wider fields of service.

Let us not find assuagement for sorrow in a eulogium upon the character of the beloved father, brother, and friend who has gone away from us, but let us talk familiarly about him. It is hard to realize that any change has come in his life, and that he is not with us yet. To speak of him as if he were dead, as if all our relations with him had suddenly been severed, and he far away and es-

tranged, would be to force the mind and the heart
out of their wonted haunts, and to compel them
into unfamiliar channels; would be to do injustice
to ourselves, our page, and to him.   Only a few
days ago we called upon him and found him, as
usual, occupying his rolling-chair, but surrounded
on this occasion with a festoon of ladies who had
severally called to pay their respects to him and
to his family.   After their departure, I said to
him that he reminded me of an old-fashioned bee-
hive, just before swarming time.   He laughed at
the conceit, but his face grew grave as he said,
" That is an odd comparison, but it may be truer
than you think."   I did not at once understand
the significance of his reply, but as he then led
the conversation back to a topic on which we had
conversed a few days before, the phenomena of
death, I have since thought that his reply con-
tained even more than he intended.   He meant
that there were indications of departure.   These
proved to be truly prophetic — and more, that the
results of a life of highest usefulness were left to
benefit and bless the church and his fellow-men.
In the conversation which followed, we recalled
and related to each other what we remembered of
the quiet sleeping away of the dying, and especially of the aged.   One instance came to mind of

a saintly man who in his last illness was impressed and troubled because of his sins, and especially with the ingratitude of which sin is an evidence. Mr. McCormick said that we ought not to carry such feelings beyond a genuine repentance, — that while sin was base ingratitude, and in this view doubly heinous, yet we ought to make it the occasion of double gratitude to God for his forgiveness. And with great force of expression, as was his wont when deeply in earnest, he said, "They are not our sins, and they do not pertain to us after Christ has taken them away. Does He not say, that He removes them from us as far as the east is distant from the west?" The conversation then fell off into a lighter tone, in which business, reminiscence, and anecdote were commingled. Mr. McCormick was full of apt and usually humorous illustrations, not a few of which have in the years past found their way into these columns. Referring to something that "The Interior" had said, which was possibly a little hasty, he took it off by saying that the paper reminded him of a gunpowder maker whom he had known in Virginia. "My powder," said the compounder of explosives, "is very good powder. It has only one fault, and that is that it is just a *leetle* too quick."

As the writer looks back mentally, over the twelve years of intimate acquaintance with him, the whole vista of memory seems to be strewn with his vigorous and apt sayings. The keenness of his mental perception was a frequent surprise. He would reach the heart of a subject and go all around it while other minds were only approaching it. His mind would be in advance of the words of those speaking to him, and he would reach and announce the result with almost unfailing accuracy from the premises afforded by one or two preliminary sentences. This clearness of perception, and power of rapid and accurate reasoning, in combination with his resolute courage and will, were the chief elements of his great success in life.

A marked trait in Mr. McCormick's character was his integrity — and there was a peculiarity about it. Like the righteous man described by David, while he changed not, though he had promised to his own hurt, yet he was very cautious about making promises. But a promise made was as good as a sealed bond to those who held it. When he said " I will," those who knew him needed nothing more, because he neither forgot nor failed to fulfill. While he would not commit himself to any undertaking without investigation, when the purpose was once formed there was no regretful looking back. Discouragement and difficulty only stimulated his determination. There was an adherence to a high purpose, not to means and methods. He was quick to toss aside an instrument when sure of a better one. This integrity of character reached down to the smaller things of life and of business — hence his word was implicitly trusted. Probably a more reliable man never lived. This strength of character consisted both in massiveness and in fibre, and it was as manifest when he lay dying as when he was in the prime of his physical vigor. While the flood of life sank and ebbed away, the broad and deep foundations of his faith and character were revealed as never before. He sought to lift his beloved ones above the sorrow, as he was lifted above the fear, of death. He was through Christ victorious, in his last struggle, and triumphed over the King of Terrors.

There was a combination of force with tenderness in Mr. McCormick's nature which appeared so often that it became a distinctive trait. No one ever went down in a conflict with him of any kind, without finding his conqueror softening his fall and immediately lifting him up. This also appeared in all things, from the friendly controversies and repartees of conversation, to the most serious contests of life. In the former, he began by begging leave to suggest, and ended by submitting it merely as his opinion, — but it would be a very mild description to speak of what came between the two in the way of fact and argument as a suggestion or a submission. There was that chivalry in his nature which made him the friend of the weaker party, even if that party happened to be his antagonist. The last business interview we had with him was in relation to a young man who had robbed " The Interior," and who was lying in jail. " If we can show mercy to him without injuring public justice, we ought to do it, for the sake of his mother."

I noticed in Dr. Marquis's address the mention of a trait which must have impressed many who were well acquainted with him : that he would plainly and candidly say to a man that which he would not say of him. This was certainly a rare trait. Most persons are content to make a virtue of saying nothing of a man which they would not say to his face. Mr. McCormick's rule, never expressed, but always practiced, of speaking kindly of the absent, and severely, if justice required it, only to the present, was as sensible as it was rare and Christian. It does one no good to speak unkindly to others concerning him — it may do good to rebuke him personally.

Though conscious of his strength, and without fear, Mr. McCormick was ever ready to make sacrifices for the sake of peace, if peace could be had on fair and honorable terms; terms honorable to both parties. No man in the Presbyterian church more longed for unity and harmony in its ranks. He was among the first to seek reunion between the northern and southern sections of the church. When it fell to his lot to organize this paper, he sought to make it a bond of union across old divisions of every kind; and when antagonisms afterward arose, he set aside all opposing counsels, and devised new measures and pledges of harmony. It was a special pleasure to him to gather the representatives of adverse ideas, or conflicting interests, around his hospitable board, and ply them with good cheer and placating suggestions. "We will bring them together, and if we cannot harmonize them before they part, it will be a wonder." Mr. McCormick was even more determined a peace-maker than he was a war-maker, and he prized his victories for peace more than his victories in conflict.

Before his rheumatic troubles incapacitated him for it, he was a skillful and graceful rider on horseback. Referring to the pleasure of which he was thus deprived, he said that when a young man, he was fond of managing intractable horses, and related an incident which occurred in Kentucky, where he had gone to introduce some machinery for the treatment of hemp, invented by his father. A young man of about his own age, where he was stopping, owned a very fine, unbroken animal of which he was afraid. Mr. McCormick offered to ride the horse home, a distance of half a mile, at noon, if his owner would ride him back. He accomplished his part of the feat, and after dinner led the horse out upon a soft lawn, mounted the rider, and let go the bits. In an instant his friend was landed a rod away from his saddle, in the grass. " I made sure that he would have a soft fall," said Mr. McCormick. All through life, he provided " soft falls " for those who were doomed to fall.

Mr. McCormick was as strong in his friendships and affections as in all else. Speaking of Dr. N. L. Rice, he paused a moment, and then exclaimed, " Oh, how I did love that man." The writer remembers an illustration of this part of his nature, which occured in the rush of work after the great fire. One evening, when he was deeply engrossed in business, at his home, then on Shel-

don Street, and a dozen or more men, the writer
among them, were awaiting their turns for an interview with him, Mrs. McCormick passed through
the parlor with her little Harold in her arms. He
dropped everything, took the babe, and became
absorbed in caressing and amusing it. His wife
finally suggested that business was pressing.
" Well, if you want me to work you must keep
that baby away from me. He would break up the
most promising negotiation in the world."

I do not know whether I ought to draw the veil
from that most sweet and sacred scene, the parting from his family. In a lucid interval — for he
fell into unconsciousness twenty-four hours before
his death — his family knelt about his bed, and he
led them in worship, and for praise sang a stanza
of that sweet, dear old hymn and melody, with
which probably few of the present generation are
familiar : —

> " O Thou, in whose presence my soul takes delight,
> On whom in affliction I call,
> My comfort by day, and my song in the night,
> My hope, my salvation, my all."

How appropriate and expressive! and how that
sweetest of the old melodies comes back to us
from the past! He had sung it often and often

in the bloom of youth, and in the prime of manhood, and now, as he was about to enter upon immortal youth, it came back to him again and
voiced his inexpressible trust and love. Then
taking the hands of one and another of his children, murmuring "Dearest one," he last took the
hand of his wife. "Dearest one of all," he said,
and so fell on sleep.

Mr. McCormick was indisposed to any ostenta-
tious display. He postponed the erection of the
solid and noble residence in which he died —
neither he nor Mrs. McCormick caring to have
anything so fine, but he said apologetically of it
that "My friends insisted that I owed something
to art and to the beauty of the city, and they
called it 'a cause,' and so I began it. For myself,
my occupancy and enjoyment of it will be very
brief." Strong and brave as that dear man was,
his cheeks were no stranger to tears, —

> "The bravest are the tenderest,
> The loving are the daring."

But I must pause. There would scarcely be an
end of these delightful reminiscences, and I have
only recalled a few from my own memory out of a
brief section of his life. His public career is familiar to the public, and some who knew nothing

of him but of his force of mind and character may have regarded him as only an embodiment of force. Twelve years of close intimacy with him revealed the precious and abundant wealth of his tender and generous heart, and sustained a profound and constantly deepening love for him. In comparison with these treasures of his soul, his wealth and world-wide fame sink into insignificance. These inner and imperishable treasures were wealth which he carried with him across the river of death. His munificent benefactions, known to the world, and his constant responses to the appeals of charity, known but to the few and the intimate — even they were but the leaves of the tree of life implanted in his soul, and which will yield its varied fruits forever, in " the land o' the leal." All that is earthly fades. Dust even now returns to its dust, and with it wealth and fame are no more to him ; but that integrity, that dauntless courage, that intellectual power, that tender heart, that magnanimous spirit — these qualities of that dear and noble soul are shining and will shine, as the stars, for ever and ever.

W. C. Gray.

[*From " The Central Presbyterian."*]

REMINISCENCES OF CYRUS H. McCORMICK.

When the historian of the future comes to speak of the great Americans who have done the most to develop the resources of their own broad, rich territory, who have offered to the whole world the greatest facilities for commercial enterprise and social intercourse, and who have succeeded the best in lightening the burdens of mankind, by the side of Franklin and Fulton and Joseph Henry and Morse, they will not forget to mention Cyrus H. McCormick. Wherever the golden wheat rustles in the breeze, the panting toilers under a hot sun will hail him as their benefactor. It is not from this standpoint, however, that I am viewing him. Others will tell of him as a mechanical genius, as a zealous churchman, as a munificent patron of secular and theological education, and as a wise, patriotic, influential, and philanthropic citizen; but now that the grave has closed over him, I would speak to others, with something of the pleasure with which I spoke to him, of certain traits of his character which struck me as valuable and attractive.

We were old friends. I knew him in his early manhood, when the idea of the great reaper seemed to us "the bee in his bonnet;" again, during his tedious waiting upon Congress for his patent; and later on, in his happy home in New York.

Unquestionably he was a man of noble intellect. The inventive faculty of his mind was not, as may have been supposed, an independent attribute, over-riding all the others, and achieving success by its individual superiority. It was but one of a number of qualities wonderfully blended, and in measure and tone and strength adjusted with such consummate delicacy and precision as to make, in their combination, what we felt to be his genius. He had logical, analytical, and executive power, an almost unerring judgment, an indomitable will, and a patience that could not be overthrown. To these was added that rare gift of mental confidence which, spurning self-conceit, and disdaining self-distrust, enabled him, with practical fairness, to determine the extent of his abilities, and estimate what he might expect from them. Within these bounds he was bold in his schemes and prodigious in his work; sparing no labor and neglecting no detail, however small, that was necessary to the full accomplishment of his wishes.

And he demanded *thorough* work; a certain integrity of purpose ran through everything he did, furnishing the key that would open his whole character and explain much in his conduct to others. He hated shams; practiced none himself nor allowed any in any of his belongings. When first visiting him in the city of New York, many years ago, I found him less interested in what was elegant and advantageous in the location and appointments of his handsome house, than in the stability of its material and the skill and finish of its workmanship. His moral nature was of the same type, in this particular, as the intellectual; his kindness and sympathy, his hospitality and loyalty, his affection and generosity were all instinct with the same principle. His religion also was pervaded by it; indeed, through the labyrinth of his whole nature this thread guided the way.

At the time of the visit referred to, he was in his massive strength, bearing the weight of an immense business. To me it seemed sufficient to exclude every other thought, yet I found he did not allow it to excuse him from important domestic cares; and I was often gratified and surprised to see how much he bore my personal pleasure upon his mind, and how constantly he was carrying out new ways to secure it; doing it all too with such delicate tact as to forbid the jar of a suspicion on my part that these attentions crowded yet more the already full routine of daily pressing duties. The thing that struck me most, however, was the religious aspect of the family, and I often remarked afterward that I had never seen children more conscientiously and successfully trained, nor the Sabbath anywhere kept with an air of greater consecration. The good old Scotch-Irish Presbyterian strictness in which both he and I had been reared in the valley of Virginia, Mr. McCormick had transplanted to his home in the rushing commercial metropolis of the Union. Of course the mother of the little family was an admirable colleague, still he did not shift upon her his responsibility, but stood at his proper post as watchman over his own household.

Subsequently we strengthened our friendship by occasional meetings, but in the summer of last year I had the pleasure of being again, after a long interval, his guest at Richfield Springs. In the intervening years violent illnesses had so far impaired his physical powers that he could no longer take a step without assistance. He was confined to a rolling chair, and moved about by a servant. After the first pained surprise at his condition, every hour brought back to me his old-time look and manner. He was eminently himself in spite of his feeble voice and constrained posture, and now, while my sympathy was ever going out to him, my respect and regard grew increasingly higher and warmer, day after day.

The religious element in his character had long been the one in which I took most interest, and had watched with most eagerness. It had run the gauntlet of oft-repeated struggle, disappointment, and failure without loss and without stain. It had been subjected to the severer ordeal of many splendid and varied successes, and come out from it clear and clean. But how will it be now, I questioned, when God has laid His hand upon him, withering his strength and destroying his physical independence. I soon found, however, that in his age and weakness the dear Master to whose service he had given his best days had not deserted him. The stalwart period of his life had passed, and with it, the hardy, aggressive Christianity that it required; and now, near the twilight, his piety had fallen into a softer, gentler tone. From out the burden and heat of his exciting day he had come into the quiet eventide of life in which " they labor too, who only stand and wait." He was thoroughly submissive under his restrictions, cheerful, unembittered, alive

to the interests of others, kind, sympathizing as
ever, and patient. "How patient you are," I said
to him once, under some unexpected manifestation
of that quality. "Patient?" he repeated with surprise, "why, it behooves me to be patient." In
his own view only the "unprofitable servant" after all! On another occasion he exclaimed, in a
sort of apologetic tone for what he considered
some shortcoming in what he was doing, "Ah,
you see I am good for nothing now!" A young
lady who, unperceived, was standing behind him,
tapped him gently on the head and whispered,
"You are all right here, at any rate." The grateful smile that lighted his face, and the tear that
glistened in his eye, was his immediate and eloquent response.

His summer home bore testimony to his exquis-
ite taste. It was in a region where nature was
prodigal of her gifts. "Open your blinds in the
morning, for the view," one of the ladies said to
me the night of my arrival. "Nothing can surpass
our Virginia mountains," was my loyal, though
unspoken retort. In the morning I rose languidly
to fulfill my promise. In a moment every sense
was alive in worshipful admiration of a prospect
from which nothing beautiful was absent. But
the master-spirit in this lovely home was the fee-

ble old man in the rolling-chair. The same wonder-working power of detail was as characteristic
of his sympathy as of his mechanical labor, and
gave him a sort of universal presence in the
house. If I had marvelled years before that a
busy man had " had leisure from himself " for the
grateful, minute cares of hospitality, I had much
more cause for wonder now, that a sick man had
so much unselfish thoughtfulness to bestow upon
the comfort and enjoyment of the large number of
widely different guests gathered under his roof.

I poorly represent his kindness if I fail to bring
to view the self-denials of it. It often taxed him
severely in time and exertion. It was not the
mere impulse of a natural endowment, and a sort
of recreation, it was the out-giving of a high-strung
principle which had been carefully cultivated by
incessant exercise. A female inventor called one
day for an interview. When the hour came he
listened to her small affair with unaffected attention, and with his strong judgment gave his counsel. It was a striking picture. There was no su-
percilious manner in the great inventor towards
the lowly one — no haughty impatience of her nar-
row talent and small beginnings, but the courtliest
courtesy and most genuine concern encouraged
her confidence and excited our admiration.

He seemed never to lose the memory of his own tussle, as an inventor, with many a difficulty and defeat before he won his victory, and always retained the warmest regard for those who had in any degree furthered or cheered him in his early undertaking. In a most unusual way he would seem to me to exaggerate the benefits he had received, as with his old vehemence he would relate some of them to me. Except perhaps, Rev. Dr. William S. Plumer, he possessed, more than any other man I ever knew, a loving sense of obligation to the friends who had served him in trying periods of his history.

I found his respectful observance of the Sabbath undiminished by his long contact with the world and its business and honors. Although during the week he never joined us until the afternoon, yet when Sunday came he was the first person ready, and his rolling-chair was waiting at the foot of the incline which he had been allowed to build from a side door of the church to the carriage-way, when his carriage reached the door. As he was rolled to a place near the pulpit, he went early, I thought, to avoid observation; for, with all his courage, he was a modest man. He enjoyed the privilege of public worship, and when so many pleasures were beyond his reach, I was truly glad that this was spared to him. At the conclusion of the service the people gathered about him with a heartiness of greeting that must have been grateful to him.

He delighted in music at all times, and often in the evening would join the circle at the piano; but especially on Sunday evening he enjoyed it, and nothing could be more pathetic than the vim with which he sang his favorite verses of the hymns, and united in the doxology.

Somewhat removed from the gay group of young people, he would talk with me of the old friends and home in Virginia. On such themes he seemed to break away from his physical shackles, and roam over the old ground with the glow and vitality of youth. The spell was but momentary. Even then, though exempted from acute pain, at any hour, his physicians thought, the summons might come. He had a keen desire for life and toiled resolutely to protect and prolong it. He had great aims he wished to accomplish, and up to the last was planning and performing much for the good of man and the advancement of the Church of God. But when death came, it found him ready for the change, and the simple sentence that reached me, " There's nothing now but heaven," had in it the tenderness of all earthly farewells, with the clear ring of a calm and assured faith.

In his long life and with his large means, he did much for his family, his country, his church, and his race; and the world is the better and the happier for his coming into it.

S. C. P. MILLER.

As the gnarled oak of stately form and size,
   With strong and sheltering and widespreading arm,
   Protecting travelers from the beating storm,
Stands forth, a giant midst surrounding trees ; —

As in the eventide, when day is done,
   The full cathedral choir their anthems raise,
   And with harmonious chant their Maker praise,
And the sweet benison of life is sung ; —

So hast thou braved the storm of passing years,
   Protecting weaker comrades in the strife ; —
   So, in the evening of thy noble life,
The harmony of thy great thoughts and deeds appears.

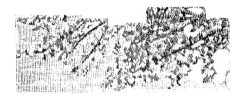

Loving Tributes.

LOVING TRIBUTES.

———◆———

PRINCETON, N. J., *May* 31, 1884.

MY DEAR MRS. MCCORMICK, — I have thought
of you and yours very often, and always with tenderest sympathy, since the news reached me that
your dear husband had passed away. I can understand how great your bereavement is, and how
heavy the blow must be, even though God in his
Providence had in a measure prepared you for it
in these last years of Mr. McCormick's declining
strength. I know too, that acceptable as sympathy always is, human words have little power to
lighten grief. God alone can heal the wounds of
sorrow.

I cannot but feel that, alike in the circumstances
of his life and of his death, Mr. McCormick has
been highly favored; and you, I am sure, must
feel, when you reflect upon his career, that gratitude has a right to triumph over grief.

It is given to few men to live a life that is characterized by all the elements of honorable success.

Such a life, however, Mr. McCormick's was. By common consent he occupies a place among the immortal names in the history of invention.

He lived to witness the successful establishment of the Theological Seminary which had been the object of his benefactions, and of whose future, even in its darkest hours, he was never known to doubt. And now, in the fullness of years, amid the sorrowful regrets of a great city, and a powerful Christian denomination, he has gone down to an honored grave.

There are elements in his life which make that life almost unique. And yet, were this all that could be said, those who loved him would find but little satisfaction in the story of his worldly successes. But this is not all, nor is it even the best that can be said; and gratifying as his career must doubtless be to you, I am sure that the feature in his life upon which you dwell longest, and in which you find most comfort now, is his persistent loyalty to God, and his unobtrusive but unfaltering faith in Christ.

What a tender, impressive manifestation of that faith was given in the closing hours of his life, when, standing upon the bank of the river which he was soon to cross, he lifted up his heart in prayer and commended his family to God! What a precious memory that last religious service must be to you and your children. May God comfort you and them. May he lead them all to love and fear their father's God; and may their lives be spared as his was, for long years of honor and usefulness.

I remain, my dear Mrs. McCormick, ever very faithfully yours, Francis L. Patton.

New York, *May* 14, 1884.

My dear Mrs. McCormick, — At length has come that for which God in his Providence has been preparing your mind, and under which His grace will sustain you. You have, you know, our deepest sympathy, but better far, you have the close, tender sympathy of Him who took our nature and knows its susceptibilities.

You will remember that your husband had the preparation of spirit required for the change, that Divine Grace had given him great usefulness, that he had been in an extraordinary degree permitted to see it, and that you have the fullest assurance now that he is with his Father in heaven, in the presence of Him whom he had trusted. There is nothing as to him over which to be depressed. There is good reason for ample joy, and for keen sympathy with the happiness of his now perfected being. His highest aspirations for himself are now realized to the full.

Praise God for all this; and, need I say it? trust Him for all the future.

Yours in the blessed truth,   J. HALL.

PRINCETON COLLEGE, *May* 17, 1884.

MY DEAR MRS. MCCORMICK, — Little did I think, when I lately spent those two pleasant days with you, that your dear husband and my friend should be so suddenly called away from us.

But the will of God be done. However hard you will be able to say so.

You will miss his society. But you had the satisfaction of waiting upon him (which no doubt was an unspeakable gratification to him) to the last.

Infirmities were evidently growing upon him, though he looked fresh when I saw him, and life could not have been a pleasure to him much longer. So God took him to himself. You cannot but mourn the separation, but you will lean on the arm of Jesus as your beloved, and thus hold on your way through the wilderness, with the earth beneath your feet, and heaven in your eyes.

He had finished his work. That reaping machine has been an immense blessing to the country. His monument will be the Theological Seminary at Chicago. I am so glad that you took me to visit it when I was at Chicago. It has won the confidence of the whole church. It is sure to be permanent. It will, centuries hence, be sending forth men to preach the unsearchable riches of Christ.

The younger children will now be entirely under your care. God will enable you to do this responsible work. Mrs. McCosh sympathizes with you. Please show this letter to your son. He will imitate his father in doing good.

Yours truly,   JAMES McCOSH.

MY DEAR MRS. McCORMICK, — As I sat in the Seminary chapel yesterday, witnessing the closing exercises of the institution, a paper was handed to me with a notice of Mr. McCormick's death. I could not hear it without a thrill of pain at the sense of my own loss, as the uppermost feeling, of a friend so kind and true and tried; one of such long standing, of such affectionate judgment of me, and whose interest in my welfare was always so warm and reliable. I have no such friend left. Some years ago a dear old friend of this same type, only more closely allied and less separated by distance, passed away, and to my feeling of bereavement was added the fact, that of such friends few remained to me. Now I have none, and the circle of my contemporaries too is fast narrowing its bounds. But however painful the parting, there is, if we be Christians, a certain and joyous meeting hereafter.

As regards my much valued friend himself, I cannot be sorrowful. He has had a life full of enterprise, of labor, of vicissitude, of struggle, and of much physical suffering. Amid much suspense and defeat, he has, in the Providence of God, been permitted to win great successes. He has by his genius and toil been a benefactor to his race. He has built up a character of rare integrity; and having been early aroused to religious convictions, has held to them with great tenacity in the face of wonderful temptations, and exemplified their power in his life, both public and private. He has testified to them too, in the generous use of his large means, and when God laid his hand upon him as in these last years, how touchingly the gentler traits of piety shone out! And now, after all these long labors, faithfully engaged in to the very last, it is all right that he should be taken to his rest.

I feel a pleasure in the thought that the toil of living, — the restless nights, the rolling chair with its many wraps, the night-watch, the cares of a great business, and the thousand tender anxieties for the family, are all over forever.

And who of us can understand what is the glory comprehended in that change, when "this mortal shall have put on immortality!"

But though it is all happy for him, yet his home is darkened, the church mourns, and many a good cause will weep its loss. But to his children, his noble character will be a greater good than his splendid genius, and his prayers and piety a richer inheritance than his estate. The older ones will know this, and the dear little boys will be taught it not only by them and you, but may, if they live, have it brought to their minds by the providences of their personal history. And thus the memory of him will grow in strength and tenderness as the years roll on.

Your affectionate friend,

S. C. P. MILLER.

PRINCETON, *May* 15, 1884.

ST. LOUIS, *June* 5, 1884.

MRS. CYRUS H. McCORMICK:

DEAR MADAM, — Do not think me unmindful of your great affliction and our common loss, that I come so late to express my sincere sympathy with you. I was on my way to the Assembly when I heard of the death of your honored and noble husband, and the circumstances of travel prevented me from doing what my heart prompted, — to write immediately. The sad tidings came to me as a great surprise; for, though he had long carried the burden of his infirmity (and with what singular patience!) I had still hoped that his great vigor, both of mind and body, would serve to continue his life for many years. But now he is gone from us, the stalwart man, so strong in will, conviction, purpose, faith, and affection. I can assure you that there is a wide-spread grief, and a deep sense of loss, throughout the country and the church, in view of his removal. And yet, what is this public sorrow to that which overshadows your own home? There, where the light of his presence is gone out, the darkness is most intense. Your heart in its loneliness tells you how much you have lost, and the slowly passing days reveal more and more the greatness of your bereavement.

But I would not, dear madam, say anything to increase your sense of sorrow and loss. The rather would I ask you to consider the things that remain for your consolation, and of which death cannot rob you. There is the memory of your husband's life, so full of manly effort and noble achievement; a life rich in blessing to the world of labor, and above all, so useful to the church. This is your possession forever, and it is a comfort to know that the world is better from the ministry of your husband.

What a rich legacy he has left to your children, — the heritage of a noble name enrolled among the benefactors of the race. Again, how sweet the comfort that, as he lived the Christian's life, so he died the Christian's death. I have been touched to tears in reading the account of his last hours, and I have rejoiced in his testimony to the grace of God. Surely you can rejoice while you weep, in thinking of the gain that has come to him through death. Hope, too, is yours, for in a "little while" you shall see him again.

Your bereavement also brings you into a new relation to God. He is "the God of the widow, and the Father of the fatherless." What gracious and loving titles does the Eternal wear for the consolation of his afflicted ones! And now it is your privilege to deal with Him by these titles. But pardon me my many words; I wish only to assure you and your sorrowing children, of my sincere sympathy, and to mingle my tears with yours over a common loss, for there has fallen "a prince and a great man in Israel." Praying God our Father to comfort you, and to keep you all in this sore trial,

I am, yours in Christ,

SAMUEL J. NICCOLLS.

My DEAR MRS. McCORMICK, — I feel as if my relations to Mr. McCormick warrant me to express my most heartfelt sympathies in your profound grief. Your husband was a gifted, large-minded, and noble, as well as a greatly distinguished man; and wielded from his invalid chair vast interests connected with the world's industry, national politics, and Christian institutions.

Our entire Faculty joins with me in this expression of sympathy with you in your bereavement and in earnest prayers for the Divine blessing on you and yours.

Very respectfully and sincerely yours,

THOMAS H. SKINNER.

CHICAGO, *May* 15, 1884.

UTICA, *June* 23, 1884.

To MRS. CYRUS H. McCORMICK:

My DEAR MADAM, — Ill health has prevented me until this late day from expressing my sorrow at the death of your husband. I held him in high regard as a man, and I valued him as a friend.

His genius and his services to the public, as well as his character, will long preserve his memory. I sympathize with you in your great loss. I hope and pray it may be alleviated by many blessings. It will ever be a source of gratification to you and his family, that Mr. McCormick's triumphs were of great value to his whole country. Few have been able to serve their fellow citizens in ways so beneficent to all classes.

I am with very great respect, yours truly,

HORATIO SEYMOUR.

CINCINNATI, *June* 13, 1884.

DEAR MR. McCORMICK, — I have read the sketches of your father with much interest. To one accustomed to regard your father's achievements in the industrial arts, and having some means of appreciating the revolutions in those arts of which he was the master spirit, there is something deeply impressive and suggestive in these testimonials, witnessing how all was surmounted by the great philanthropic and religious enterprises to which his mature thought and strength were dedicated; and how the same wisdom, energy, and firmness of purpose directed and wrought success out of these enterprises.

His life is in so many worthy aspects representative of the century, three-fourths of which it spanned — a century distinguished above all others for its inventions, its material progress, and the extent and variety of its charities — and it so thoroughly illustrates the harmony between the largest business success and persistent and conscientious philanthropy; between the faculty which utilizes material agencies and the faith which recognizes divine supremacy; between the self-reliance which commands men and the humility which worships God — that it affords a rich theme for memorial discourses, one especially fitting to be presented before the students of the colleges which are indebted to him for endowments.

In the course which begun among the hills of the Old Dominion, and was finished in the high places of the metropolis of the New Northwest, there must have been such contrasts of light and shade, and such association with events of critical historic interest, as to furnish the materials for a very vivid and thrilling picture — a succession of prophecy and realization, instructive and inspiring.   Yours sincerely,

ROBERT H. PARKINSON.

CHICAGO, ILL., *May* 18, 1884.

MRS. C. H. MCCORMICK:

DEAR MADAM, — You have my warmest sympathies in your bereavement. It is no doubt a source of gratification that he was such a practical friend to the human race, and has been so acknowledged on every side by those who know it best, since his death. Of the many things accomplished by him are the following: —

I. By his inventive genius the burden of gathering the harvests of the world has been made lighter for millions of men and women, and has afforded the toiling masses good bread at low prices, who would otherwise have been obliged to eat coarser and poorer food.

II. By his patronage of the press and institutions of learning the world is more enlightened, and consequently there is more real joy and less misery.

III. By his liberality to the church, he has been enabled to help in great measure in the extension of the kingdom of Jesus Christ among men. Thousands will rise up to call him blessed for offering the means to provide the gospel for them when they needed it.

IV. And better yet, as the Master said, " Rather rejoice that your name is written in the Lamb's book of life." No doubt his name was written there, and that he heard that welcome plaudit, " Well done, thou good and faithful servant," etc.

May his mantle of service fall upon you and his children, and may you all be possessed of a double portion of that spirit with which he served his God and the world. The time is but short when you and yours will be called to meet him. The Lord bless and keep you, and grant you a long life of usefulness and joy in his service.

Yours in Christ,

ROBERT WEIDENSALL.

HOT SPRINGS, ARK., *June* 12, 1884.

DEAR MRS. McCORMICK, — I cannot let the sad hour of your life pass away without adding my word of sympathy to the thousands which you have received throughout the country. The death of your husband may be in a manner likened to a national calamity. By his genius he lifted the burdens from the shoulders of thousands, made food abundant, and reduced the danger of death by starvation. Wherever civilization has advanced McCormick's Reaper is known, and his machines have done more to elevate the human race than any invention of the day, as there can be no progress without first making *food cheap* and *abundant,* and the reaper has done more for the tiller of the soil than all other inventions combined. I feel that you can be congratulated upon having been the wife of a man who has done so much for his race, who has left such a bright mantle of distinction upon his children, and who died full of honor and full of years. He had lived out the measure of his life fully and completely, — who could, who would do more? My relations with him, as a physician and as a friend, were extremely cordial. With all his aches and pains and infirmities so trying to the nervous system, I found him always the same courtly, urbane gentleman. I cannot recall a single unpleasant episode in our intimate association. My entire family unite with me in warm greeting to you and yours, with the assurance that none more cordially, more heartily wish you happiness than we.

With high regard, sincerely your friend,

A. S. GARNETT.

MRS. CYRUS H. McCORMICK.

53 BROADWAY, NEW YORK, *May* 14, 1884.

MRS. CYRUS H. McCORMICK, CHICAGO:

MY DEAR MADAM, — I am sure you will credit me for earnest sincerity when I assure you of my heartfelt sympathy for the loss of your most excellent husband, distinguished alike for his public usefulness and his private virtues.

It has been with me the regret of years that you gave up your residence in New York, by which I was deprived of the opportunity of the social intercourse which I so much enjoyed during the period of his sojourn in this city.

You and his family have reason to be proud of his career, which has left its mark upon the history of our nation's rapid progress in material prosperity, in furnishing the most important stepping-stones in the march of our agricultural prosperity by which our national wealth has been increased by untold millions, and at last he has fulfilled his happy destiny, and full of years, and with an unblemished reputation, he leaves naught but pleasing memories behind.

With the assurance of my sincere regard, I remain, yours faithfully,   AUSTIN BALDWIN.

Mrs. E. D. JUNKIN writes, —

I recall with great pleasure the only time I saw your dear lamented husband, at our home, then at New Providence Manse, Virginia, when he called near to our dinner hour. I pressed him to dine with us, — he declined, asking "only for a cup of cold water," and making some such pleasant remarks about those words of our Saviour as to make a lasting impression upon my mind.

HENDERSON, KY., *June* 19, 1884.

MY DEAR MRS. MCCORMICK, — Will you allow the old missionary from Kentucky to mingle his tears of sympathy and sorrow with you and your loved ones in your desolated home? I have not, I never can forget those delightful visits and the cordial and hearty welcome received at that happy home on Fifth Avenue, New York.

I can still see the large, loving heart mount into his face, and hear the cheering words of your late husband, now, alas, hushed in death. I have never met Brother McCormick without feeling better, happier, and nearer our heavenly home; indeed, his whole life *was a benediction*, but he is called up higher and has received a *starry crown.*

I need not tell you, my dear madam, that there is only one place for bereaved ones to go with their sorrows and sufferings: we must go and tell Jesus. He alone can pour the balm of consolation into our bleeding and broken hearts.

> " In every pang that rends the heart,
> The man of sorrows had a part,
> He sympathizes with our grief,
> And to the sufferer sends relief."

18

" Blessed are the dead which die in the Lord from henceforth : Yea, saith the Spirit, that they may rest from their labors: and their works do follow them."

> "Rest, rest, rest, brother, rest!
> Sweet thy repose on Jesus' breast,
> Battle all fought, and victory won,
> Tearful we say 'God's will be done!'
> Rest, brother, rest."

Praying that the shadow of the Rock of Ages may be around you and yours, I am your sympathizing friend, JOHN McCULLAGH.

38 EAST THIRTY-THIRD ST., *May* 16, 1884.

I need not tell you, my dear friend, that our hearts are with you in your deep affliction. I would I could utter some word of comfort to you and to your children. The infinite Father, in whose bosom your husband rests, best knows how to console you.

An eminent writer, alluding to a loss similar to your own, says, " For the first sharp pangs there is no comfort! Whatever goodness may surround us, darkness and silence *will* hang about our pain."

I know this to be true; and yet, even in the

first days of overwhelming sorrow, there is a certain consolation in the " clinging companionship with the dead," and in the careful gathering up of all that remains of him, in our own memories and in the memories of our friends. We run backward along the path we trod with him, and pick up the gems he scattered on the way. Nothing seems small or trivial. Everything is sacred.

While I write to you I remember so many little things, all tending to illustrate the tender side of Mr. McCormick's character, expressions dropped by the way of pity for the infirm, of devotion to his mother's memory, of love unutterable of his own immediate family. I remember the earnestness with which he said to me, " I feel anxious to keep my children together and make them feel dependent on each other. It is painful to me to think of divided and scattered families."

He cherished a picture of his mother, and once calling my attention to it said, " It is a good face, — a strong, honest face." Talking of flowers one day, he said, " I love the old-fashioned pinks because they grew in my mother's garden in Old Virginia."

The first time I ever saw him was in the little Presbyterian chapel in Washington. My husband pointed him out to me, expressing his own interest in the invention which was then new to the world, and his faith in its final success. The strong, firm face, the attentive manner during the service, are still fresh in my memory. I knew him well when he was in the prime of his life ; when he had realized all he could desire of honor and success. Then, as always, he seemed to me singularly free from ostentation, and from desire for outward " show and circumstance." He eagerly sought, for himself and his family, influences of the highest Christian character.

I recall with tender appreciation my interviews with him, at intervals, during the last four years of his life, of many kind expressions toward myself and my children, of esteem and friendship for my husband, of gratitude for the smallest attention or service rendered him. The last time I saw him was during his last visit to New York. Feeling very sad to see him so ill, I expressed, as I leaned over his chair, my regret and sympathy. He looked up at me kindly and replied, " It does seem hard, — it *is* hard, — but I have great comfort in ejaculatory prayer." It was this that enabled him to triumph over mortal pain, and preserved, in its vigor and clearness, the mind, which, to the last, was able to guide great interests, industries, and beneficent enterprises.

Remembering those large interests, I feel that my own record is of very little moment. I have only brought a tiny gem or two, as setting for the grand central jewels of his crown. Others will doubtless record the brilliant achievements of a long life. I love to dwell on his great and tender heart, his true and affectionate nature.

Writing of him thus he has seemed very near! He passed away so gently we scarcely realize he is gone. It was not death, it was translation! One moment he was here with a prayer on his lips for you all, the next moment he had passed away " out of darkness into light, out of dumbness into song, out of weakness into strength, out of pain into serenity."

Nothing comforts the soul so much as the hope of reunion with our beloved dead. As the disciples talked with their Divine Master, a cloud received Him out of their sight. But in answer to their upward gaze a comforter was sent to them with assurance of reunion to their lost friend.

We also, with mortal, tear-dimmed eyes gaze upward! Alas, we cannot pierce the cloud, but none the less is the promise ours that nothing is lost of those we have loved; that for them and for us, all is ordered by a wisdom that errs not, and a love that cannot be unfaithful. " They have passed into the presence of God and of His Son. *We* are immortal upon the earth until He calls us. And as the infant rests upon its mother's bosom and knows no fear; as the star swings in silence upon the mighty will of God, and knows no tremble in all its structure, so our minds may rest upon this assurance of the Divine wisdom and love, and remain in infinite tranquillity and peace." Sincerely yours,

SARA A. PRYOR.

"HE BEING DEAD, YET SPEAKETH."

MAN toils to be remembered ; spire and dome,
And monumental hands outstretched on high,
And marbled speech of glories that have been,
And pages eloquent with storied wit,
The moving splendor of harmonious song
Conspire to cry aloud : " Remember me,
O living men, remember me who died."

But one has lived who raised no carven shrine
To blazon forth the splendors of his name ;
Who hewed no crimson monument of slain
With conqueror's sword ; whose speech was not for fame.
He overcame his fellow-men by good
In generous strife ; and in the gentle spring,
When the broad hillside smiles with tender green,
When golden summer glows along the plains,
And waves the rustling billows of the grain,
The wide earth utters forth his message then,
The message sung on Galilean hills
To watching shepherds, " Peace, good-will to men."

His name is written in the springing grain,
His message whispers in the rustling fields ;
His praise the chorus of the harvest song ;
A prince of nature and a prince of men,
A royal steward of the Blessed King ;
His garnered bounty fed the lord and serf,
Mankind has been his guest ; what wonder now
Mankind is sad when he is laid to rest !

E. P. DAVIS.

CPSIA information can be obtained
at www.ICGtesting.com
Printed in the USA
BVHW082042191118
533509BV00024B/1131/P